ICONISM
Designing Modern Icons and Pictograms

GINGKO PRESS

Designing Modern Icons and Pictograms

First Published in the USA and in Europe in 2020 by

GINGKO PRESS

Gingko Press, Inc.
2332 Fourth Street Suite E
Berkeley, CA 94710 USA
Tel: (510) 898 1195
Fax: (510) 898 1196
Email: books@gingkopress.com
www.gingkopress.com

Gingko Press Verlags GmbH
Schulterblatt 58
D-20357 Hamburg / Germany
Tel: +49 (0)40-291425
Fax: +49 (0)40-291055
Email: gingkopress@t-online.de

ISBN 978-3-943330-52-6

By arrangement with
Sandu Publishing Co., Ltd.

Copyright © 2020 by Sandu Publishing
First published in 2020 by Sandu Publishing

Sponsored by Design 360° — Concept & Design Magazine
Edited and produced by Sandu Publishing Co., Ltd.
Book design, concepts & art direction by Sandu Publishing Co., Ltd.

Chief Editor: Wang Shaoqiang
Executive Editors: Katherine Ye, Anton Tan
Copy Editor: Kim Curtis
Designers: Huang Zhiyi, Pan Yuhua
Sales Manager: Deng Baoyi

Cover Design: Pan Yuhua
Front and back cover projects by Kolektyf

info@sandupublishing.com
sales@sandupublishing.com
www.sandupublishing.com

All rights reserved. No part of this publication may be reproduced or transmitted in any form or by any means, electronic or mechanical, including photocopy, recording or any information storage and retrieval system, without prior permission in writing from the publisher.

Printed and bound in China

CONTENTS

006 PREFACE

➲ VISUAL IDENTITY

017	**Interview with Kissmiklos**	046	JA Minds
019	Guggenheim Museums and Foundation Rebranding Concept	048	Hotel El Call
		060	SF Design Week
022	Kaposvár City Branding	050	Weihai Design Valley Architectural Space Poster
024	Pléz		
026	Pet Plate	053	Solcellskollen
028	Guerewol Festival 2019	054	Dimple Contacts: A Clear Vision for Change
030	Yashin&Partners		
032	Hanbok Culture Week	056	Eva Candil
034	Przetwory Creative Design	057	Vistto
035	Antaeus Travel Group	058	Zveropolis
036	Barcelona City Works	060	Matstreif
038	Ô JAPTHAï	062	Trulia
040	Lololand Family House	064	MINOA
042	TEDxKoenigsallee	066	8th Olhar de Cinema
044	26th Istanbul Akbank Jazz Festival Campaign Identity	068	MokaClube

070	Shoushan Zoo Visual Identity Redesign	092	My 10 Most-Liked Hong Kong Architecture of the Century
072	Styrad	094	Azerbaijan Tourism Forum
074	Tero	096	CREATED IN MOLDOVA ♥ APPRECIATED WORLDWIDE
076	Lidl—20 Stories	098	Kindergarten & School Saulės Gojus
077	Dohop	100	Yours Truly
078	Addressable	102	Exovo
080	Cross & Corner	104	Esquinita Inka
082	City Express Plus	106	Foxtrot Delivery Market
084	Canon—Imaging for Good	108	Avo Consulting
086	Adidas Iconography Rebrand	110	Croissant Café & Bakery
088	FRESH BLOOD DG YOUTH	112	Pollution and Drought Episodes
089	liv		
090	mu objek		

⊙ WAYFINDING

121	**Interview with Yoshiaki Irobe**	150	Inbound League
123	Yayoi Kusama Museum	152	Fremtind
126	Sukagawa Civic Center tette	154	S5
128	Mediateka in Tychy	156	Sentralen
130	Atenció Skater	158	Airport Iconography Proposal
132	Vega Scene	160	Vessel Hotel Campana Susukino
134	Signage Sports Hall Bitzius	162	Museum of Józef Piłsudski in Sulejówek
135	Nijinoki Nursery School		
136	ZUCZUG Head Office Sign Design	164	Nowy Targ Office Building in Wrocław
138	Volksschule Edlach		
140	MEDIATEKA Culture Spot	166	Medic-r
142	Simon Wayfinding	167	Saint-Paul Hostel
144	Unidad Educativa Particular Marista	168	Container Hotel
146	Madison Shopping Center	170	Casa Museo Wayfinding ID
148	NInA	172	S/PARK
149	National Stadium in Warsaw	174	La Casa Encendida

176	BUSS by Allianz	188	Takao 599 Museum
178	Hot Yo Studio	190	The Feluma Theater
180	De Krook	192	Istanbul Kultur University
182	Signage for Augusta Raurica	194	The Software House Office
183	Adana Archaeology Museum Wayfinding Design	196	Santander
184	The University Children's Hospital of Kraków	198	Kimitsu City School Lunch Cooking Facility
186	New's To-O	200	17th FINA World Championships Budapest

➔ INTERACTIVE DESIGN

209	**Interview with Tom Birch**	233	Kakao Corp
211	Re·view App	234	Sunday
214	eat to be_	236	Aqer
216	Connected	237	Nommi.net
218	The Darwin Challenge	238	Sooner
219	Good Pair Days	240	Tofu Design Website
220	Pro-Aktiv	242	Rakfice
222	Callibri	244	DNB Lærepenger
224	Bankin iOS App Design	245	SBI Bank App
226	Servo Delivery—Laundry App	246	KNVB—Royal Dutch Football Association
228	RIDE M.E—Movable Enjoyment	248	Made X Made—Website
229	BeeBetter—Habit Tracker App		
230	WATERFLOW		
232	TucomunidApp		

249 INDEX   **256 ACKNOWLEDGMENTS**

PREFACE

Nicklas Haslestad
Creative Director,
Scandinavian Design Group

An icon or a pictogram is, arguably, the most effective single piece of graphic design. It could easily be the most important part of a brand identity system. Creating iconography programs requires a lot of work and an immense eye for detail and craftsmanship.

I have reason to believe that my first encounter with icons and pictograms was back in 1994 when Norway hosted the Olympic Winter Games in Lillehammer (I was four years old). Those sport icons were designed using a technique inspired by Norwegian rock paintings to represent the various sporting events. They emphasized the vision of humanity in the Olympic ideal and underlined the connection of the Norwegian people with their own historical roots. Those icons were used *everywhere*—on all kinds of merchandise, clothes, flags, commercials and wayfinding systems. The symbol of a torchbearer from the 1994 Olympic Winter Games was even cut into a 40-acre area of forest on a hillside near Lillehammer. To this day, you can see it when skiing the slopes in Hafjell. That is—I believe—a successful iconography program. Regardless of its dimensions, scaling from a few pixels on a 4:3 TV screen to 40-acre area of forest, it is recognizable as the 1994 Olympic Winter Games in Lillehammer.

Since then, technology has advanced considerably, and we are now able to create more complex digital and interactive icon libraries. There is no doubt the world of the user interface would be boring without icons. All great apps use icons frequently and consistently. Without exception, icons simply make both the user interface and overall experience better. Today, we even have easy access to beautiful and functional ready-made icons. It is a great alternative indeed, even though nothing beats a custom set. Meanwhile, it is interesting to think about the future of icons. Especially within virtual reality, icons will play a prominent role to make an easily understandable experience.

Scaling from our fingertips to architecture, wayfinding systems are synonymous with icons and pictograms. Imagine an airport without them. Imagine a festival without them. Imagine a highway without them. Imagine a hospital without them. Icons in wayfinding systems make them easier for everyone to navigate and understand. This is also why a good icon should be cut to its bone without any unnecessary detail.

A solid iconography program can be crafted to perfection and work across all media. Often developed from complex grid systems, good icons are consistent and full of identity. Icons are either good or bad. There is no middle ground. The Italian designer Massimo Vignelli said it right: "Quality is when you know that you have reached a high level in your work, when it really sings, when it touches you, when it responds. Quality is a level of intellectual elegance that is unmatched in other forms." Icons and quality go hand in hand.

When I got into the graphic design profession, I was introduced to the German graphic designer and typographer Otl Aicher, who was, arguably, best known for having designed the iconography for the 1972 Summer Olympics in Munich, Germany. Those pictograms had an everlasting impact on the design industry. The use of stick figures in the iconography proved influential to public signage around the world and possibly—in one way or another—to some works in this very book.

Icons explain things. They make people laugh, they make them cry, they are a means of interaction and, from time to time, they change people's lives and the world around us.

VISUAL IDENTITY

A visual identity is made up of different graphic elements, including icons. In this chapter, various projects will show that icons can not only represent the brands' beliefs, but also communicate with consumer audiences directly.

010

TRANSPORTATION

Simple Small Icons: Ground Transportation
Design/ **Icons8, Marina Fedoseenko**

Travel
Design/ **Indielogy**

INTERNET AND TECHNOLOGY

Smart Technology Line Part 1

Design/ flat-icons.com

COMMODITY

Muji Icon Design
Design/ **Yunjung Seo**

IKEA Icon Design
Design/ **Yunjung Seo**

FOOD

Food
Design/ **Smalllike**

Vegetable and Fruits
Design/ **Bearfruit Idea**

LANDMARKS

Asian Capital Landmarks

Design/ **József Balázs-Hegedűs**

Landmarks of France

Design/ **József Balázs-Hegedűs**

TRAVEL

Travel and Camping

Design/ **Turkkub**

Travel and Transportation Icon Pack

Design/ **Kanda Euatham**

BUSINESS

Auction
Design/ **Siwat Vatatiyaporn**

Modern Business Icon Set
Design/ **iStar Design Bureau**

Interview with
Kissmiklos

Q: Can you please share with us your background? How did you get started as a designer?

A: I finished my studies as a painter at the Hungarian Academy of Fine Arts. About a year later, when I created my first logo design, a friend told me "do not touch a computer, it is not your way. Go back and keep painting." I became very angry and started to work on more logo designs. When I first visited London, I saw the Victoria and Albert Museum's logo. That was the moment I decided to create a logo no worse than that. A few years ago, an architect friend told me: "I'm at least as bad as a graphic designer, as bad as an interior designer you would be." Then I started to engage in interior design. When I look back, anger always guides me through the important steps of my career or rather desire shows that I can do other things. I am currently changing and I think the next step for me is to return to fine art.

Q: What do you think are the key attributes of great icon design?

A: Proportions, coherence, a unified visual appearance and connection with the rest of the identity are very important.

Q: How does icon design affect the visual identity of a brand? Let's take your design as an example.

A: I usually design the visual identity first and then the icons. If you look at my Guggenheim rebranding, my icon design reflects the font I used.

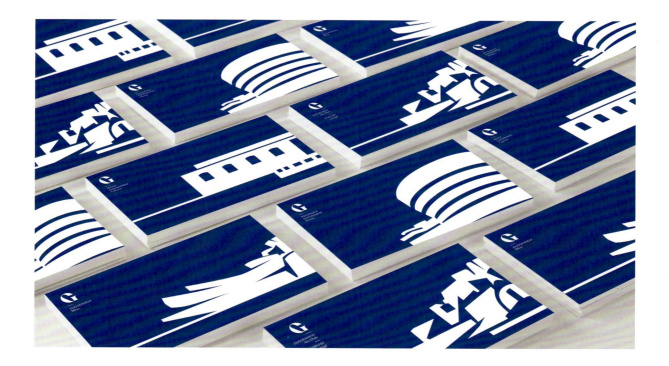

Q: What's the process you go through when designing a set of icons for a brand?

A: I determine what icons are needed. Then I start experimenting with proportions and style. Meanwhile, I pay attention to the connection with the other elements of the whole identity. I make many variations, then choose the best from the final ones. I look for solutions, for uses. I make compositions with them. I upgrade the icons, if needed, and finalize them.

Q: The project Guggenheim Museums is a rebranding concept. You used the iconic silhouettes of the landmark Guggenheim building as the identity. How did you come up with such an idea? And why did you use International Klein Blue (IKB) as the main tone?

A: The Solomon R. Guggenheim Museum, designed by Frank Lloyd Wright, has a very iconic shape. Many designers have already processed this silhouette. The Guggenheim Museum Bilbao, designed by Frank Gehry, is so unique that the museum is a symbol of an entire city. I like my design identity to be based on a strong concept. I also like the background information. I chose IKB as the main color for the identity concept as a reference to Yves Klein's works in the Guggenheim Museum. Klein developed and used this blue in many of his paintings and registered the paint formula. It was a very defining moment in the history of modern art.

Q: We know you tried to give a contemporary look to the Guggenheim Museum. Can you explain more about your design strategy to make this happen?

A: Initially, I did the research. I wanted to know everything about the museum's background and the current identity design. I built the concept with the combination of relevant information and modern contemporary art history. I wanted to design a strong iconic logo. One of the most powerful things in this design is the vivid blue color. This is a very important and clever part of the visualization. Many art lovers recognize it as IKB. Meanwhile, humor is also an important part of the design, especially in the way of the presentation.

Q: You have been working in different fields like architecture, fine art and graphic design. That's interesting, but also challenging. What do you gain from working in these fields?

A: Yes, it is challenging. But from a certain point of view, I am a perfectionist and always want to create the best work I can. I need to control every part of the project, to be sure that the concept I imagined can materialize at every level. I love to work in different visual areas. This fills my mind with fresh ideas all the time.

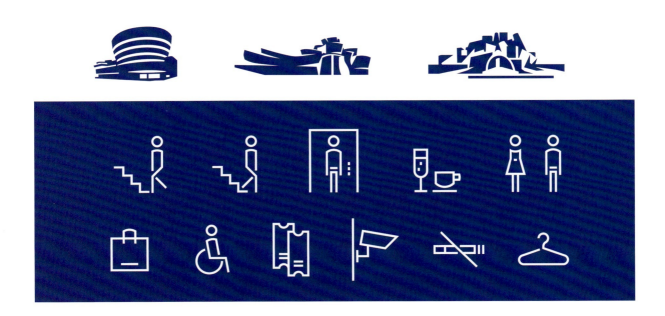

Guggenheim Museums and Foundation Rebranding Concept

Design/ **Kissmiklos**
Photography/ **Eszter Sarah**

This project is a rebranding concept for Guggenheim Museums and Foundation. Kissmiklos created a new logo and identity for Guggenheim. While the logo is almost based on the typeface Verlag, it is the main font in the identity, but he switched the logo "G" to Abbott Miller's curving "G" as a continuity of the existing design. The identity consists of silhouettes of the landmark Guggenheim buildings, which he also believes are central to the Guggenheim's great brand. The main color is International Klein Blue as a reference to Yves Klein's blue swimming pool at Guggenheim Bilbao.

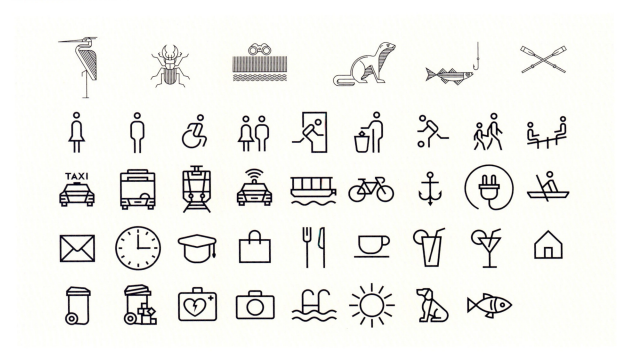

Kaposvár City Branding

Design/ **Kissmiklos**
Photography/ **Eszter Sarah**

Kaposvár is a city in the southwestern part of Hungary. Kissmiklos intended to help people understand why visualization is important and how he can make a countryside city much more attractive and exciting. To create a strong and historical concept of this branding, Kissmiklos got inspiration from the famous Kaposvár-born painter, József Rippl-Rónai. His favorite zinnias are the inspiration for the color of this branding. Meanwhile, Kissmiklos designed a set of icons, referring to wildlife in Lake Deseda in Kaposvár and city's center daily life.

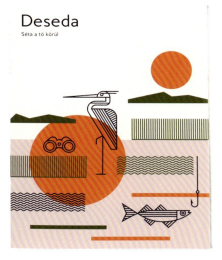

Pléz

Design/ **Kissmiklos**
Photography/ **Eszter Sarah**

Pléz is a Budapest-based café and sandwich shop chain. Kissmiklos designed this new visual identity by extracting elements from French pastry and English take-away food shops.

Pet Plate

Design Agency/
Sagmeister & Walsh

Pet Plate is a direct-to-consumer brand that delivers fresh-cooked meals for dogs. One of Pet Plate's main objectives was to show they serve human-quality dog food. With this in mind, Sagmeister & Walsh took inspiration from the traditional blue and white decorative plates that have roots in cultures all over the world. They balanced the fine line illustrations with bold, funky typefaces and humorous copywriting to establish a playful tone of voice.

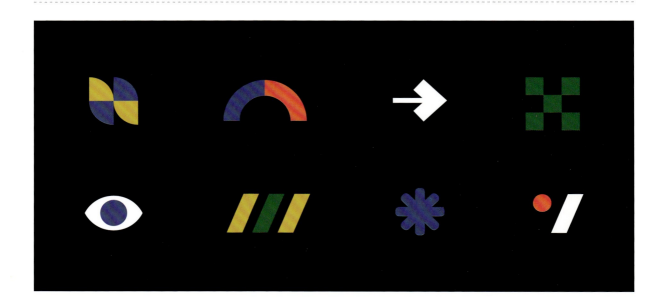

Guerewol Festival 2019

Art Direction & Design/ **Kenneth Kuh**

Guerewol is an annual courtship ritual competition among the Wodaabe people in Niger. The purpose of this project was for the world to get a glimpse of Wodaabe culture. Wodaabe tribal characteristics were further expanded into a logomark that resembles a welcoming smile. Dressing up, applying make-up and performing courtships were the inspiration for this design. It is a seven-day experience carrying no social stigma or moral restriction intended to liberate everyone's soul for a brief moment.

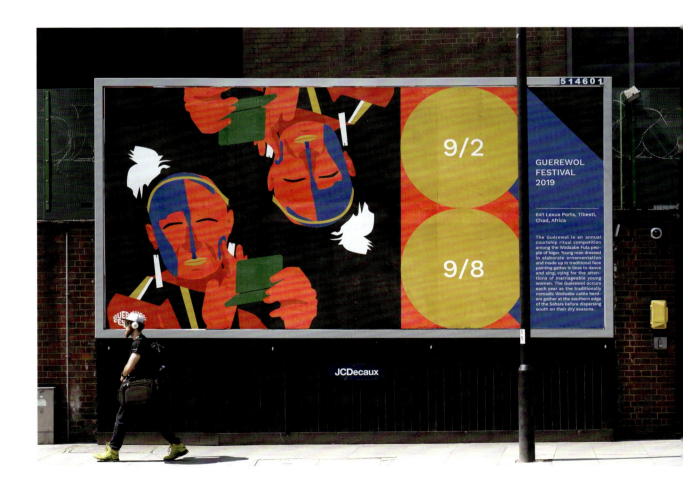

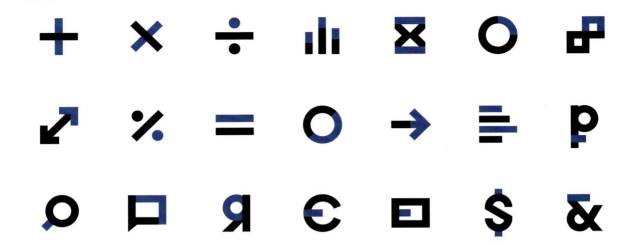

Yashin&Partners

Design Agency/ **Mountteam**
Creative Direction/ **Tigran Kazaryan**
Design/ **Tigran Kazaryan, Kristina Talova**

Yashin&Partners is an accounting company that is rapidly developing and breaking the stereotypes of the industry, demonstrating that accountants are not always moody and boring. According to this company concept, Mountteam designed a rebellious identity and website for it. What's more, the relevant icons, such as mathematics and currency symbols, show the characteristics of the accounting industry.

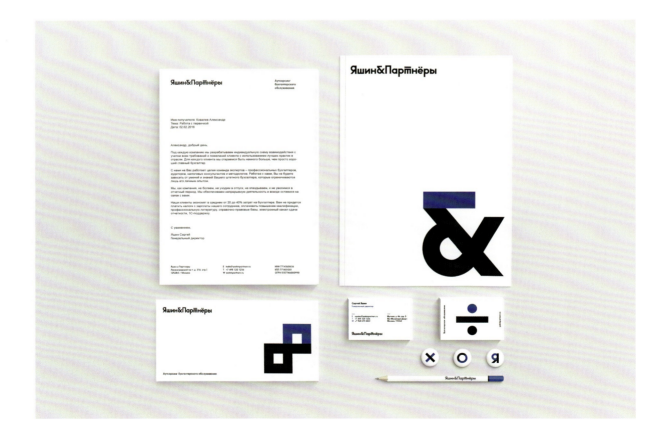

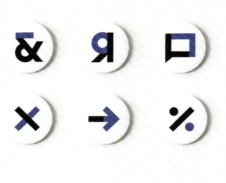

Hanbok Culture Week

Design/ **Tyodi Hyojin Lee, Hyunwoo Kim**

Hanbok Culture Week is a brand to arouse people's interest in traditional Korean clothing, *Hanbok*, and to publicize its industrial and cultural values, globally. The icons are designed to show colorful and dynamic features of the brand by visualizing various parts of traditional Korean clothes, such as *jeogori* (upper garment), skirt, lucky bag, *beoseon* (socks), *gat* (hat) and folding fan. They are used in different materials related to Hanbok Culture Week.

Przetwory Creative Design

Design/ **Aleksandra Lampart**
Client/ **Przetwory Creative Design**

Przetwory Creative Design is a project created for extraordinary people who value the individuality and beauty of everyday objects. Each project of Przetwory Creative Design has its own story, combining minimalism with functionality and retaining the exceptional attention to details. The new logo contains the history and key of the brand. A new color palette, a series of illustrations, a graphic system on social media and strong typography have created the new unique character of Przetwory.

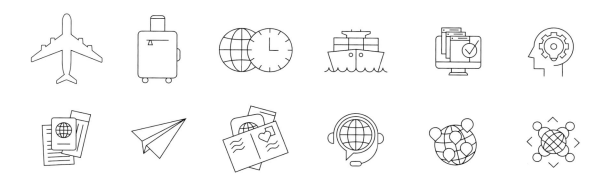

Antaeus Travel Group

Design Agency/ **Busybuilding**
Creative Direction/ **Dimitris Gkazis**

Antaeus Travel Group is a global maritime travel agency. The brochure Dimitris Gkazis designed contains all the necessary information about the company—its services and contact information. Meanwhile, the sales representatives can use this leave-behind brochure for meetings with new clients. Dimitris designed a special corporate identity with bold typography and a series of icons inspired by the world of travel and transport. The brochure reflects the client's character and values as well as the specialized services and assets that make Antaeus Travel Group stand out from its competitors.

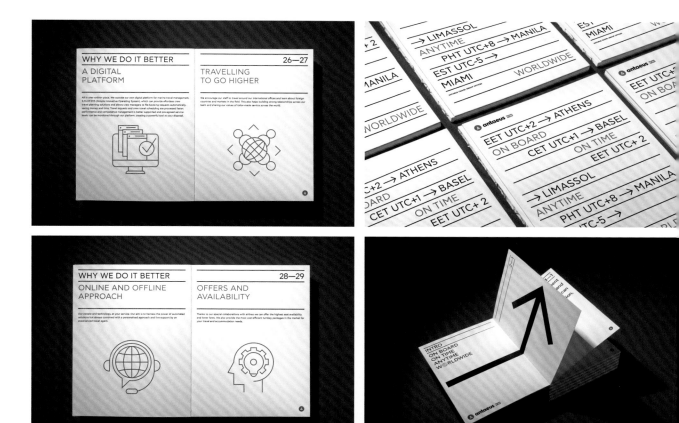

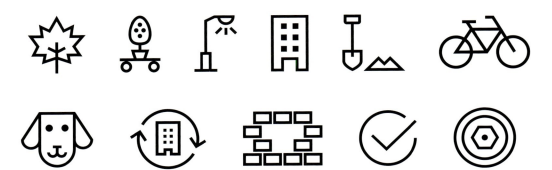

Barcelona City Works

Design Agency/ **Familia**

Familia was commissioned by the Barcelona City Council to renew the graphic system for the municipal works. The main target was to display urban improvements in the form of icons that relate to citizens and function as signs. The new graphic proposal explains that the municipal works are being performed and gives citizens information about the final purpose: a bike lane, street lighting improvement, and so on. In this way, citizens can learn about the end result before it's finished.

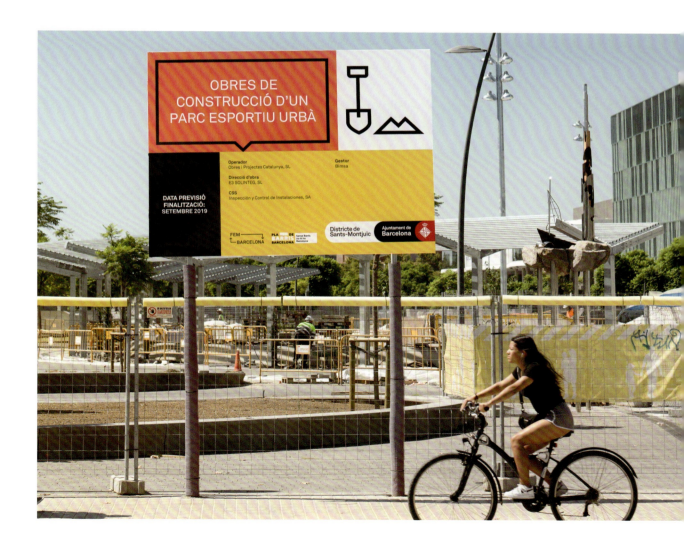

Ô JAPTHAÏ

Design Agency/ **BIS Studio Graphique**
Design/ **Lilian Chevallier, Hugues Carrere, Franck Magnabal**
Client/ **Ô JAPTHAÏ**

Ô JAPTHAÏ is a restaurant that provides traditional food based on Japanese and Thai cuisine in a lounge atmosphere. BIS Studio Graphique worked on the visual identity with an aim to create an image combining the Japanese and Thai graphic design spirits. The main color of the project refers to the flags of Japan and Thailand. The logo and icons reflect the spirit of the essence of the design and cuisines of Japan and Thailand.

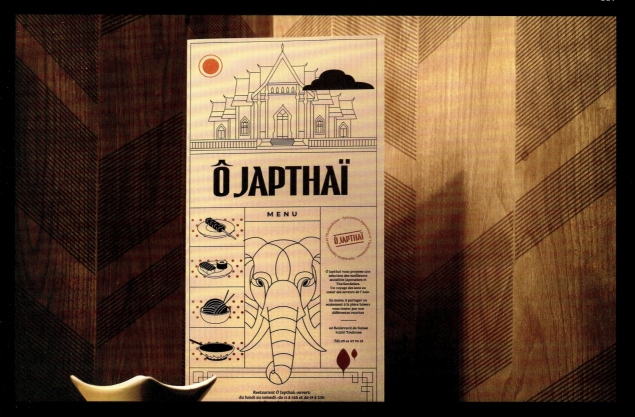

Lololand Family House

Design Agency/ **ReflexDesign**
Art Direction/ **Suning Lan**
Creative Direction/ **Yi Cai**
Design/ **Jie Zhang, Xi Pan**
Photography/ **Zhenghao Wu**

Lololand is a family house created by the fashion corporation LOTI. To keep childishness and imagination, ReflexDesign used a very simple design to show fun and creativity with punctuation marks. The "!" and "*" represent the shiny, childlike and happy parent-child time. The designers created a super-strong identity and an extensive system with this unique expression around the restructure of symbols, animals and digits to fulfill the different demands from apparel, home furnishings and food.

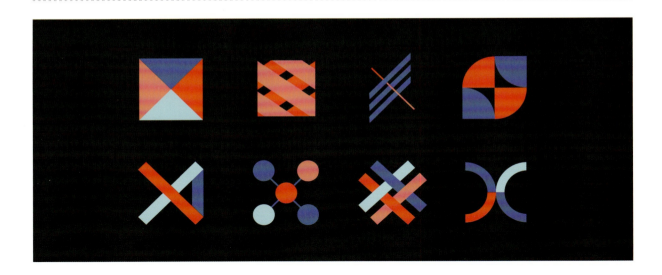

TEDxKoenigsallee

Design Agency/ **KittoKatsu**
Photography/ **KittoKatsu**

TEDxKoenigsallee was the first official TEDx event that took place in Duesseldorf, Germany. Under the theme "The Future of...," 10 international speakers were invited to present their views on diverse topics like religion, happiness, epigenetics and so on. The identity for the event reflects the unknown prospects as well as the challenges and possibilities of the future through a series of 10 different X's, one for each topic and speaker.

26th Istanbul Akbank Jazz Festival Campaign Identity

Design Agency/ **TBWA Istanbul**
Art Direction & Design/ **Yiğit Karagöz**
Creative Direction/ **Arkın Kahyaoğlu**
Client/ **Akbank Jazz Festival**

Jazz is a fusion of rhythms and cultures. It is improvised, authentic and full of passion like the city of Istanbul. For the latest ad campaign of the Akbank Jazz Festival, TBWA combined jazz with Istanbul. The designers created pictograms by combining icons of Istanbul with the tagline "Jazz state of the city," which has been used for a long time. They designed eye-catching visuals from a combination of Istanbul icons and jazz instruments and created a variety of icons compatible with advertising media.

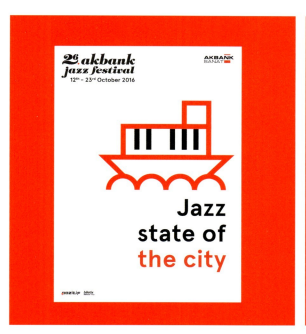

JA Minds

Design Agency/ **6D-Kco., Ltd.**
Art Direction/ **Shogo Kishino**
Design/ **Shogo Kishino,**
Nozomi Tagami
Client/ **Minds Agriculture Cooperate**

This easily understandable pictorial design represents JA Minds' wide range of services in the Tama area of Tokyo. In the process of the icon design, the team realized they needed to show the relevant services simply. The icons can be swapped and customized based on the location where the signage is set up.

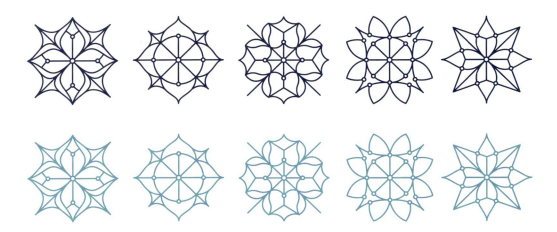

Hotel El Call

Design Agency/ **Studio Wete**
Creative Direction/ **Santiago Rama**
Illustration/ **Studio Wete**

Hotel El Call is one of the oldest hotels located in the gothic quarter of Barcelona—a cultural meeting point on the shores of the Mediterranean Sea. Different gothic vaults of cathedrals were used as a reference. Meanwhile, a system of illustrations was created to generate an endless number of graphic pieces. One of the main pieces of the hotel identity is the logo, which can appear in different ways, according to the media. Studio Wete has also created a series of pictograms using the same style and some room numbers.

SF Design Week

Art Direction/ **Kenneth Kuh**
Icon Design/ **Xiaocha Zhang**

SF Design Week is an important weeklong, citywide festival that showcases the unique intersection of ideas, design, business and entrepreneurism that make the San Francisco Bay area a birthplace of the future. By participating in the event as a design intern in SYPartners, the designer created a complete visual system around the speakers to make sure everything tied to the topic "Thinking to Make" and to introduce people not only to the concept of the prototype, but to SYPartners as a brand.

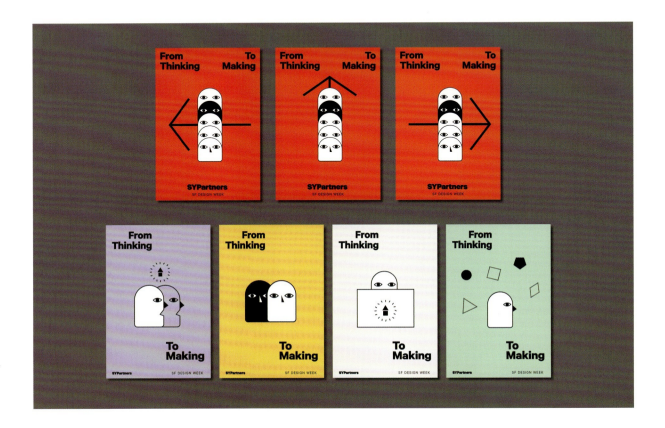

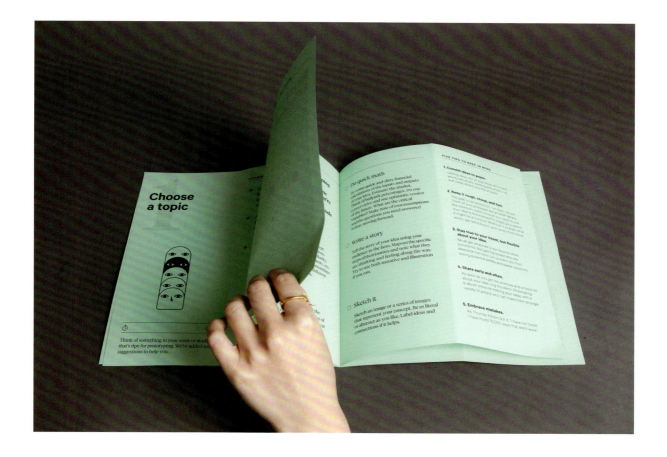

Weihai Design Valley Architectural Space Poster

Design Agency/ **3% Design Studio**
Design/ **Xiongjun Deng**

Weihai Design Valley was built in a valley. It covers an area of about 330,000 square meters. The posters were based on cave painting and used simple lines and words to describe different wild animals and plants and they encourage people to pay attention to the natural ecology outside the valley.

Solcellskollen

Design/ **Gustav Karlsson Thors**

Solcellskollen is a price comparison website for solar power systems. The icons are based on simple geometric shapes that come from the elements of solar power systems—the sun, the house and the electricity, which is also the inspiration for the identity's color palette.

Dimple Contacts: A Clear Vision for Change

Design Agency/ **Universal Favourite**
Creative Direction/ **Dari Israelstam**
Design/ **Meghan Armstrong**
Client/ **Dimple Contacts**
Styling/ **Jessica Johnson**
Photography/ **Jonathan May, Benito Martin, Lynden Foss**

Dimple is Australia's first direct-to-consumer contact lens subscription service. Universal Favourite set the foundation for this vibrant, human-centered brand. The branding taps into a flaw in existing contact lens' blister packs, creating customized patterns for each prescription number and displaying them boldly on the blister packs. It is significantly easier for users to identify the pack that's specific to each eye when they're not wearing their lenses.

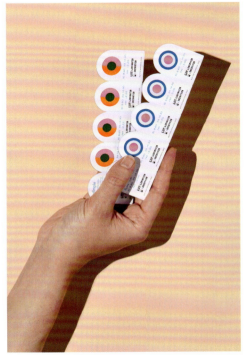

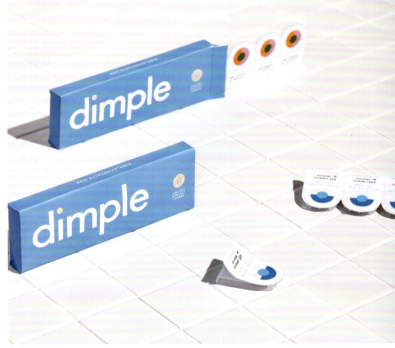

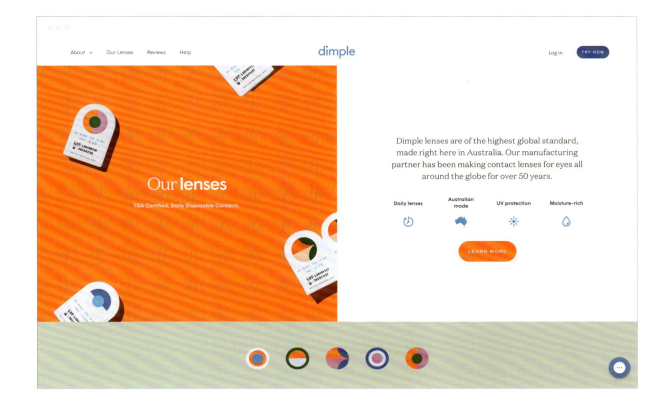

Eva Candil

Design Agency/ **Un Barco**

Eva Candil is a musical proposal that addresses the diffusion of popular music of different genres and styles. Inspired by the popular culture of Argentina, Un Barco developed a whole visual identity to match Eva Candil's concept—using some of the most easily recognizable features of different music genres.

Vistto

Design Agency/ **The Woork Co**

Vistto is an architecture studio helping architects and clients visualize their ideas on paper. The Woork Co designed a strong logo, which is much closer to the construction world. Meanwhile, they transformed those materials and resources, which are accustomed to an architecture studio, into icons. Some of them are represented as patterns in monochromatic prints.

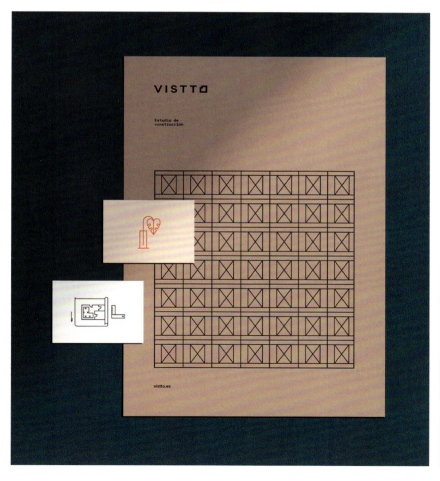

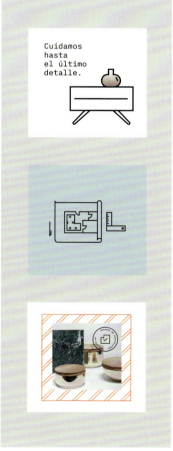

Zveropolis

Design/ **Christina Boletus**

Zveropolis is an online store for pet products. Its owner is a young, hip-hop fan who has a leading YouTube channel dedicated to pets and interviews with breeders. This brand is designed for the teenage target audience.

Matstreif

Design Agency/ **Scandinavian Design Group**
Design/ **Vetle Majgren Uthaug,
Nicklas Haslestad**
Type Design/ **Robin Mientjes**
Photography/ **Marthe Thu**

Matstreif is a food festival that takes place in Oslo, Norway. This identity aims to be visually striking in both Oslo and throughout Norway. It's filled with life, taste, humor and energy. As a frame of reference, the designers found inspiration in the established music festivals. The farmers are put in the center and become rock stars for the weekend. They have included ingredients to hit all people's senses. A vibrant and flexible identity constantly changes tastes, textures and pace.

Trulia

Design Agency/ **DesignStudio**

DesignStudio worked with Trulia to renew their brand. A new strategy and mission was developed and translated into a meaningful, neighborhood-centered brand identity. Motivated by the idea of creating a visual language based on a world of neighborhoods, not only the homes inside them, DesignStudio took creative inspiration from map iconography. Just as neighborhood communities are made of many parts brought together in interesting compositions, they designed a suite of unique icons that evoke the charming uniqueness of a neighborhood's dwellings, environments and amenities.

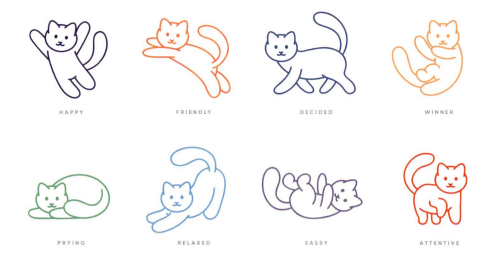

MINOA

Design Agency/ **Platform 64 Design Studio**
Design/ **Murat Celik**
Management/ **Evren Akozbek**
Client/ **Minoa London**

MINOA is a London-based, cozy bookstore for people who love cats, coffee and books. The cat is a key element in the design. The design team created a set of eight icons with orange, purple, green and blue colors. Meanwhile, they vividly display different poses in the icon set. The overall design is cute, playful and colorful.

8th Olhar de Cinema

Design Agency/ **Pedro, Pastel & Besouro**
Creative Direction/ **Eduardo Rosa, Gustavo Caboco**
Design/ **Dora Suh, Felipe Lui, Fernanda Corrêa, Lucia Angélica, Rafael Ancara**
Client/ **Olhar de Cinema**

The concept of the 8th Olhar de Cinema Festival is a "storm," which reflects the current political and social situation in Brazil. The design team's starting point was a redux of the 1960s Tropicalia movement, which fought against the country's military dictatorship with a creative and colorful protest. Inspired by those modern typefaces, red spaces and pictorial freedom, the design team created a rebellious style for the festival.

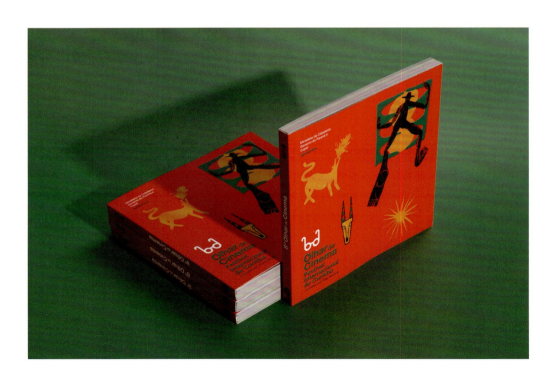

MokaClube

Design Agency/ **Pedro, Pastel & Besouro**
Creative Direction/ **Eduardo Rosa, Gustavo Caboco**
Design/ **Dora Suh, Felipe Lui, Fernanda Corrêa, Lucia Angélica, Rafael Ancara**
Client/ **Moka Clube**

The coffee brand MokaClube asked the design team to create a new visual identity. They extracted and mixed the basic elements of the Brazilian urban and countryside. They captured the rural essence of the farms and sheds where the coffee is processed. The illustrative icons allude to those elements presented in the country lifestyle, creating an illustration pack that expresses the true art of coffee making.

Shoushan Zoo Visual Identity Redesign

Design Agency/ **Project On Museum**
Creative Direction/
Jay Guan-Jie Peng
Art Direction/ **Stella Tai-Yun Shih,
Jay Guan-Jie Peng**
Illustration/ **Shing-Ying He, Yu-Chen**
Client/ **Kaohsiung Design Festival**

Project On Museum used the keywords of mountain, homeland, residence and nature to create a new logo and develop a series of graphic elements of animals and wayfinding systems for the Shoushan Zoo.

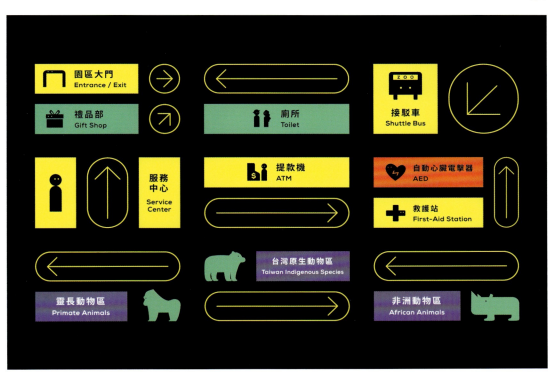

Styrad

Design Agency/
Nofrontiere Design GmbH
Design/ **Alexander Egger**

Styrad is an activity led by the Styrian government in Austria, which focuses on active communication and raising awareness of participation in cycling. The design concept establishes the bicycle as a strong, individually configurable means of transport and bundles the diverse group of cyclists into one collective movement. The designers have done this by designing two wheels to rotate constantly, taking on new shapes and setting out a playful, friendly identity that is accessible to a diverse target group. This allows people to get around by bicycle, not as an obligation, but as a fun alternative.

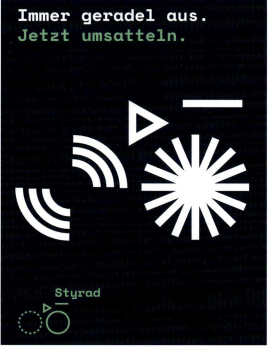

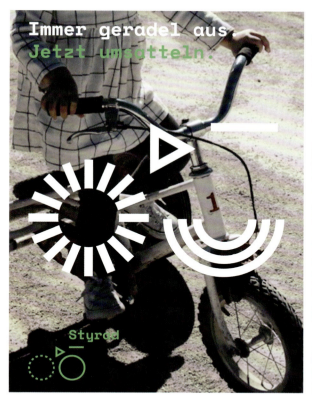
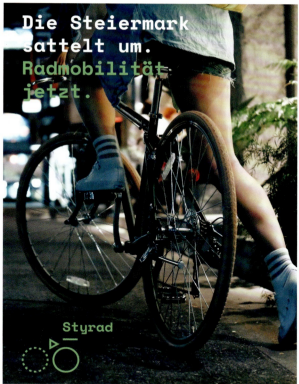

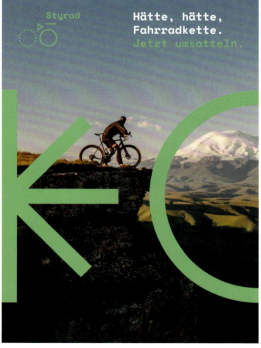

Tero

Design Agency/ **Firmalt**

Tero is an on-the-go coffee shop inspired by the distinctive neighborhoods of Mexico City. Because Tero is based in this city, Firmalt designed an element that would harness all its quirks and traits. The wordmark of Tero has a bold and strong type while the logo gives the brand a bold personality and acts as a baseline to counteract the craziness. The iconography of Tero has a bizarre style. The set of surreal icons portrays the crazy side of Mexico City, such as cigarettes, ducks, balloons, cars and high heels.

Lidl—20 Stories

Design Agency/
Caparo Design Crew
Photography/
Theodosis Georgiadis

Lidl is a global discount supermarket chain. The brand decided to celebrate its 20th anniversary in Greece by introducing a locally-produced Syrah-Merlot premium wine. Caparo Design Crew was asked to brand and name it. It was the storytelling aspect of the wine that the studio wanted to bring to the surface. To do so, the studio decided to reinvent the bottle of wine, so it could serve as both a vessel for a sophisticated liquid and its own engaging story.

Dohop

Design Agency/ **Bedow**
Client/ **Dohop**

Dohop is a flexible search engine. It pushes further to make a boring service into an attractive one. Dohop's logotype is flexible in that it can communicate things, destinations and people. Their new tagline "Anywhere Simple" is illustrated by a series of icons describing the simplicity of using the service—clicking and enjoying.

Addressable

Design Agency/
the branding people

Addressable is a brand with a vision to deliver the right message to the right person. The design team created a classic and unique aesthetic, paired with a vintage feel and the old-fashioned way of writing a letter. Taking classic cartoons as a point of reference, the studio generated modern illustrations and a linear universe for its iconography that represents old-school postage. With an adapted color palette reminiscent of traditional mail colors, Addressable steps into the future, while staying true to tradition.

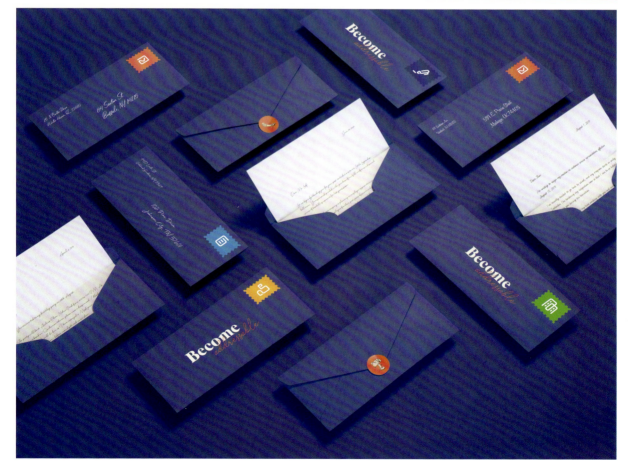

Cross & Corner

Design Agency/ **Touch**
Typeface/ **Grilli Type**
Photography/ **Al Ferrier**

Cross & Corner is a bar and restaurant in a popular day-to-night neighborhood destination. Touch's task was to design its visual identity. As a nod to the venue's location, the designers from Touch created a simple logo using a heron—a familiar and often spotted local bird from nearby Water of Leith in Scotland. For items across the venue, they created a modular grid of icons inspired by the surrounding area and what is on offer. These elements could be re-shuffled, re-arranged and re-scaled to work across several different applications.

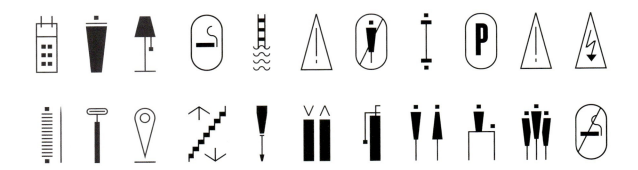

City Express Plus

Design Agency/ **Futura**

City Express Plus is an international hotel chain. Futura was in charge of designing a signage and iconography system that works with the new spaces. For the design, they thought of an experience that creates an emotional bond between the guest and the hotel without losing the unique corporate value of the brand. For the graphic, simple iconography was used, along with a modern and readable typeface that causes an impact.

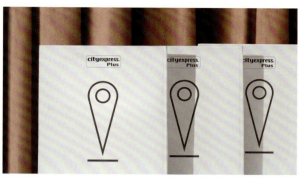

Canon—Imaging for Good

Design Agency/ **Pengguin**
Client/ **Canon Hong Kong**

Canon Hong Kong hosts a lot of CSR projects to fulfill various objectives and to target different segments in the community. Imaging for Good is a branding campaign. The logos and icons were created by combinations of the camera's lens and winking eyes, greenery and flowers to express the brand values. The whole set of icons represents positive energy to the audience.

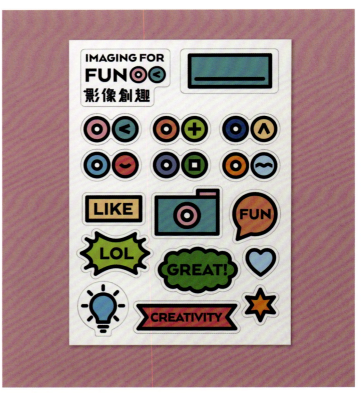

Adidas Iconography Rebrand

Design/ **Frida Medrano**

As a school project, Frida Medrano created an icon set based on Adidas. She analyzed the brand's main characteristics. Since it is sportswear, she gave inclination to the icons with a diagonal grid to represent movement and action. She took the logo as an aesthetic inspiration and made linear icons. They had incorporated the three lines from the Adidas iconic logo. She designed the icons for editorial use and exported them as a font for easy use. For the editorial, she tried to make the icons prominent to compensate for the lack of photography.

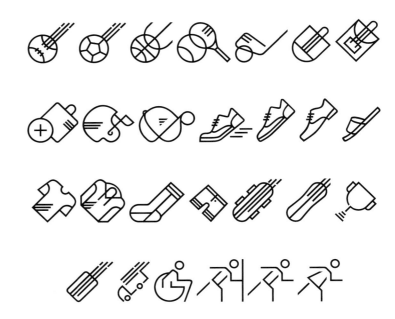

FRESH BLOOD
DG YOUTH

Design Agency/ **XIEXIE DESIGN**

This design was inspired by popular vegetable markets with the theme of cultural innovation and fresh supply. Six examples of Dongguan (DG) specialty food—sausages, bananas, beef, rice dumplings, fresh fish and roasted goose were used to represent the six cultural youths, colliding and blending, reflecting the young, fresh culture and the city of Dongguan.

liv

Design Agency/ **My Creative**
Brand Strategy/ **Alex Ostroff**

To improve liv as an approachable brand in Queens, New York, My Creative explored various directions that pushed the envelope, including playing with vibrant colors, leaf textures and watercolor art. Finally, fresh minimalism helped communicate the health and quality of the products. Along with simply designed compostable packaging in a bright open interior space, My Creative easily conveyed liv's brand value.

mu objek

Design Agency/ **Wander**
Art Direction & Design/ **Wik Kee Y.**
Client/ **mu objek studio**
Photography/ **DG Yap**

mu objek is a Malaysian brand that is constantly creating both functional and aesthetically pleasing home decor and lifestyle products with a fresh perspective and creativity. Wander created a logo that illustrates the lifestyle products that mu objek offers. The logo was then used individually to represent the various series of the products. The idea of a self-stamping name card and silkscreen bag was proposed to resonate with the nature of this handmade brand.

 Light Series 電燈系列

 Pot Series 植物盆系列

Volca
Product 小品
LS001
Colour 顏色
White 白
Light Series 電燈系列

Toothy
Product 小品
LS002
Colour 顏色
Mix 混
Light Series 電燈系列

Potto
Product 小品
PS002
Colour 顏色
Mix 混
Pot Series 植物盆系列

Giant
Product 小品
PS001
Colour 顏色
White 白
Pot Series 植物盆系列

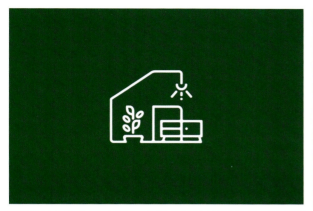

My 10 Most-Liked Hong Kong Architecture of the Century

Design Agency/ **studiowmw**
Creative Direction/ **Sunny Wong**
Design/ **Sunny Wong, Caspar Ip**

As a city with a rich historical background, Hong Kong offers a unique combination of architecture. Hong Kong Architecture Center selected 100 iconic buildings as an appreciation of the beauty of Hong Kong's architecture. To create an updated impression of Hong Kong's architecture, studiowmw transformed the 100 buildings into icons sharing the same visual language and generating an interesting visual impact from the original informative context.

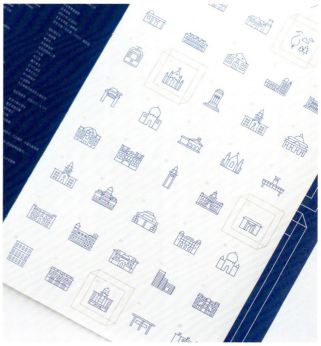

Azerbaijan Tourism Forum

Design Agency/
Meteor Advertising Agency
Design/ **Ulkar Nasibova**

To highlight the Azerbaijan Tourism Forum, Ulkar Nasibova sought inspiration from Azerbaijani cultural traditions, such as carpets, Armudu tea, gobustan hieroglyphs and kebab to create simple icons. Ulkar stated that Azerbaijani carpet is remarkable because it has absorbed the spiritual experiences of the people and aestheticizes the idea of the absolute. Its relevant, simplified icon also communicates this.

CREATED IN MOLDOVA ♥ APPRECIATED WORLDWIDE

Design & Art Direction/ **Marin Gorea Jr.**
Cooperation/ **Prior Media (Advertising)**

Marin Gorea Jr. launched this design project in three languages (English, Romanian and Russian) to display a brand-new, friendly and natural image of the Republic of Moldova. Marin stated that his creative starting point was the same letter C in three languages. Because the logotype contains many words, Marin decided to transform representative local products into icons that can combine with the logotype.

Kindergarten & School Saulės Gojus

Design Agency/ **Imagine Branding Studio**
Art Direction/ **Aistė Jakimavičiūtė-Biakauskė**
Design/ **Ugnė Balčiūnaitė**

Saulės Gojus is a bilingual school that combines different elements—urban environment, nature and knowledge. To illustrate them, Imagine created a set of playful icons. The visual identity is full of colors—a direction was chosen to distinguish the three parts of the educational establishment: kindergarten, primary and secondary schools. The organic elements emphasize the synthesis of different things: the communality, diversity of the world and uniqueness of the children.

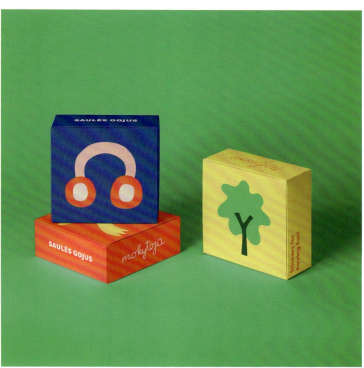

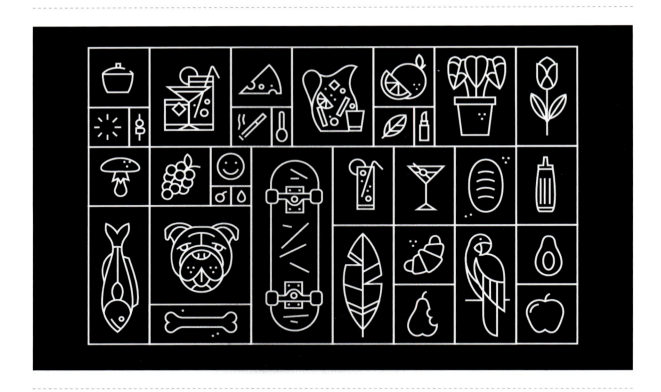

Yours Truly

Design/ **Hanno van Zyl**
Client/ **Yours Truly**
Photography/ **Ian Engelbrecht**

Hanno van Zyl was commissioned by Yours Truly to create a new identity. Hanno's solution was to create a visual language that allows for endless variation as long as the basic principle of a single black line was adhered to, along with simple and minimal typography and graphics. Although seemingly ubiquitous, this simple guideline allowed the client to completely own this visual space, thanks to thorough and extensive roll-out over various platforms and materials.

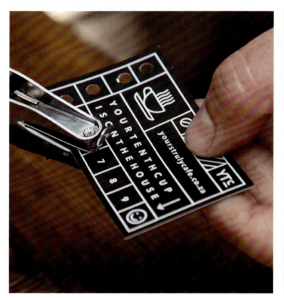

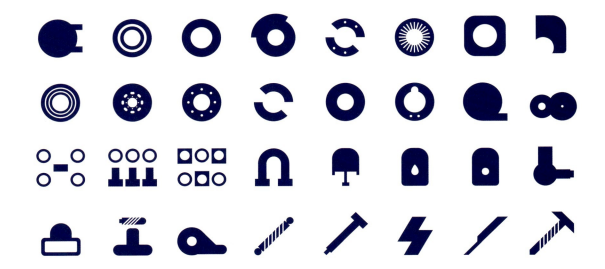

Exovo

Design Agency/ **Repina Branding**
Client/ **Exovo**

Repina Branding was asked to upgrade the corporate identity and packaging for Exovo. After researching the competitors, Repina set themselves three conditions for the new design: avoid the rigid images of auto parts in the form of 3D, real photos and complex schemes; use bright and pure colors to increase awareness on the shelf in auto parts stores; develop a scalable corporate identity and adaptive system for any packaging format.

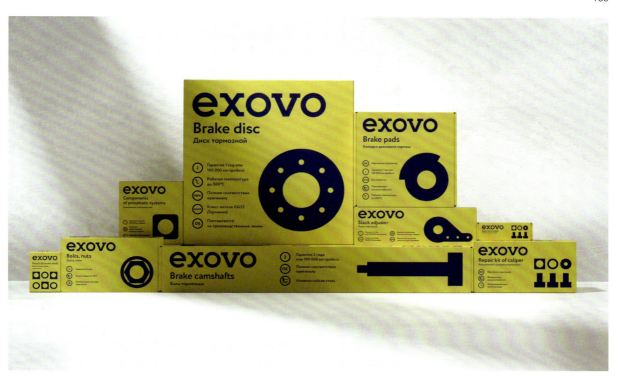

Esquinita Inka

Design/ **Antonay**

Antonay designed a brand for a Peruvian restaurant in Sabana Norte, Costa Rica. Before starting this branding, Antonay researched and used the Incan culture and Peruvian fabrics as inspiration. Antonay displayed different Peruvian animals via icon design. The overall design blends symbolism and fun.

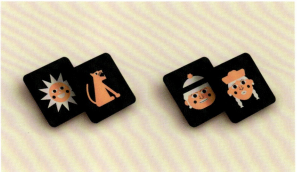

Foxtrot Delivery Market

Design Agency/ **Perky Bros**
Client/ **Foxtrot Delivery Market**
Photography/ **Brett Warren**

As a new kind of corner store, Foxtrot asked Perky Bros to design a unique visual identity. Perky Bros was inspired by the visual language of neighborhood markets, corner stores and bodegas. Fruit stickers and the comics motivated Foxtrot's new illustrations and color palette. They looked for the utilitarian typography that reminded them of letterboards and receipt printers in a neighborhood market. Overall, they wanted the elements to feel local, familiar and fun.

Avo Consulting

Design Agency/ **Bleed Design Studio**
Creative Direction/ **Svein Haakon Lia**
Design/ **Halvor Nordrum**
Management/ **Marie L. Steen**
Strategy/ **Christoffer Nøkleby**
Client/ **Avo Consulting**

Together with Avo, Bleed developed a custom typeface, Avodings, inspired by dingbats. While the original dingbats had their heyday when bandwidth couldn't support images and illustrations online, Avodings created the visual ideas of Avo's activities. While the *A* is always constant, the *v* and *o* take different shapes and are interpreted freely.

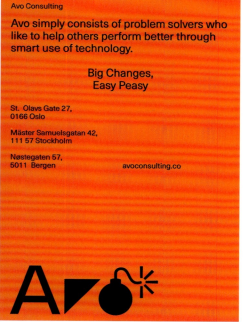

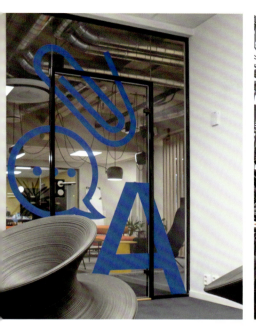

Croissant Café & Bakery

Design/ **Dave Arustamyan**

Dave Arustamyan created a visual identity for a Canadian croissant company with a flawless, but warm French style. Dave was inspired by the company's café-bakery which is located on the lake and designed a croissant-like boat as a basic graphic. Meanwhile, Dave chose the Neutral Grotesk and a seven-color palette to arrange unique and friendly images with simplified figures and graphics.

Pollution and Drought Episodes

Design Agency/ **Forma**

The Barcelona city council, Catalan government and Barcelona metropolitan area worked together to create a set of public signs to alert the citizenship about pollution and drought in Catalonia, Spain. Forma was commissioned to design the visual system to make it highly understandable and quickly executable.

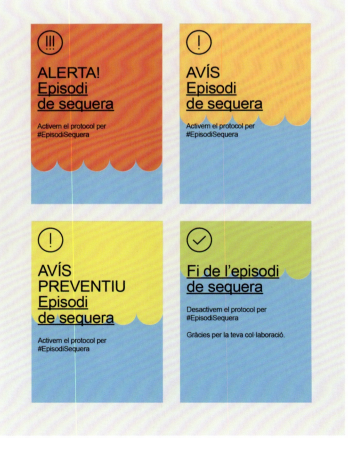

WAYFINDING

Custom iconography is a key part of wayfinding. The icon's geometric or illustrative forms can be used to communicate across ages, languages and cultural barriers. They create a consistent visual system.

WAYFINDING

Naples Subway Wayfinding System
Design/ **AURØRA Design**

WAYFINDING

Galeria Młociny—Shopping Mall in Warsaw
Design/ **Kolektyf**

WAYFINDING

Museum of Cursed Soldiers and Political Prisoners

Design/ **Marta Gawin**

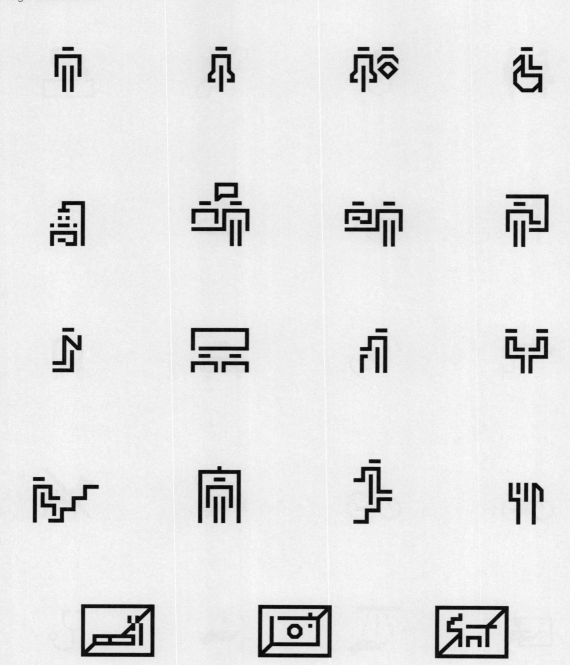

WAYFINDING

UNISOCIESC
Design/ **Firmorama**

118

WAYFINDING

Wayfinding Icon System
Design/ **Chiara Marchiori**

Signika Icons
Design/ **Anna Giedryś, Peter Machaj**

WAYFINDING

Colégio do Espírito Santo

Design/ **André Panoias, Miguel Muralha**

WAYFINDING

Trensurb—Urban Train Wayfinding System

Design/ **Cristian Garske, Cristina Carnelos, Lucas Corrêa, Lorenzo Stello**

Interview with
Yoshiaki Irobe

Q: Would you like to share some stories of you and your studio? How did you get started as a graphic designer?

A: I joined the Nippon Design Center (NDC) after graduating from the Tokyo University of the Arts. About eight years later, I got an offer as an individual designer for clients, which led to having my own team inside NDC. At the beginning of 2011, I was the only team member. Now, we are a team of six designers, including me and a project manager.

Q: As we know, icons play an important role in wayfinding design. However, words or graphics are more frequently used in wayfinding design instead of traditional icons. What do you think of this phenomenon?

A: Otto Neurath, the proponent of the Isotype, said: "What can be clarified in the pictogram doesn't need to be in words. On the other hand, there are things difficult to be drawn as a pictogram which can be easily explained in words… You have to find out which language is the best for the purpose." It means that pictograms and letters have different orientations. Pictograms are weak at conveying detailed settings and nuances, but good at transferring rapid and rough information. Also, they can be communicated beyond the boundary of language.

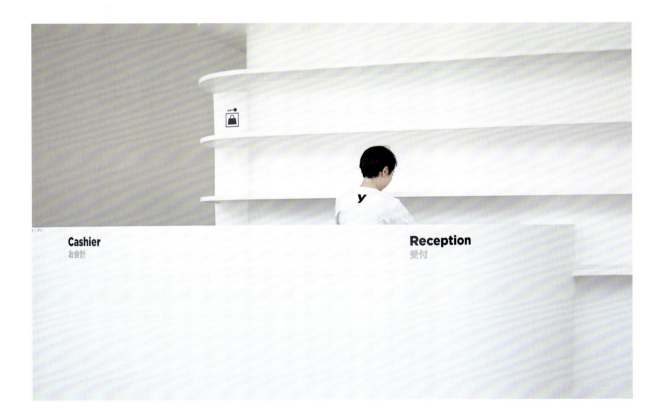

Q: The wayfinding project for Yayoi Kusama Museum carries a minimal visual style, which is somehow in contrast with the style of Yayoi Kusama that most of us are familiar with. How did you come up with such an idea?

A: The style and expression of Yayoi Kusama are different, but I think they reflect her strong and kind spirit. Also, visual identity and typography don't need to exactly match the contents, like the title letters of the artist's work collection. The visual identity of this museum is designed as if it was a device to bring out or enhance its individuality.

Q: In recent years, you have made many wayfinding systems for public spaces, including the Yayoi Kusama Museum, the Ichihara Lakeside Museum and so on. What do you think are the key attributes of a great wayfinding system?

A: There are two major values that the signage system for public facilities can provide. The first value is the guidance function and visibility. It depends on different environments. Signage systems need to be strong and sharp when requiring immediate action to guide a large number of people, like in airports, train stations and stadiums. Meanwhile, in some specific places, such as museums and hotels, signage systems need to guide people in a slow pace. The second value is that the signage system has a special design tailored to the characteristic of a facility. The signage system is the "voice" of a facility that invites people inside. It is important to select the textures, pictograms and typeface that match the facility.

Q: What would you do before designing signage for a physical environment or building?

A: First of all, we research the characteristics of the space, materials and purpose. After research, we will provide custom-made sign designs rather than pre-made ones for the space, from pictogram to materials.

YAYOI KUSAMA MUSEUM
草間彌生美術館

Yayoi Kusama Museum

Design Agency/ **Irobe Design Institute**
Art Direction/ **Yoshiaki Irobe**
Design/ **Moeko Yamaguchi,
Sayoko Matsuda**
Client/ **General Incorporated
Association Yayoi Kusama Foundation**
Photography/ **Shintaro Ono,
Riko Okaniwa**

Yayoi Kusama Museum is a branding project for the private Museum of Yayoi Kusama, an avant-garde artist. This visual identity was based on Yayoi Kusama's handwritten signature and the pictograms were inspired by her drawings.

Q: Graphic design is different from fine art. By following the requirements of customers, the designed works tend to be commercial. How do you balance creativity and the demands of your clients?

A: We always value the requests of our clients, but also focus on the requests of our users and recipients in a balanced manner. The value as creation is important, too. If the value of your creation is compromised as a result of being too close to your wishes, the job may work, but you will lose your value. Therefore, we try to fulfill the needs of clients, users and creators as high-dimensionally as possible.

Q: You have been involved in different areas of design like visual identity, wayfinding, packaging and so on. What's your plan in the field of design?

A: Recently, on-screen media such as digital signage, websites and SNS have been efficient. The most effective approach for on-screen media design is to add motion. Now, we have deep contact with users in various media such as visual identities, maps, pictograms and posters in dynamics. I am enjoying this new situation and challenging myself.

One way
館内一方通行

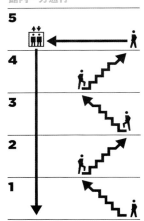

For safety reasons, please access the higher floors using the elevator or the stairs. When descending, please use the elevator.
Please be informed that in the event of inclement weather, the 5th floor may temporarily close for the safety and comfort of our visitors.

階段またはエレベーターで1Fから順番に上の階へお進みください。安全のため、階段のご利用は上りのみとし、下りはすべてエレベーターをご利用ください。
天候等により安全が確保できない場合は、5階を閉館いたします。予めご了承ください。

Visitor Policies
ご観覧にあたって

 Please do not touch works on display or display cases.
展示作品、展示ケースにはお手をふれないでください。

 Photography and filming are not allowed except for areas with permission signs. No flash photography or video. No tripods or selfie sticks.
写真・ビデオ撮影はできませんが、一部撮影可能な場所には表記がありますので、従ってください。ただし、フラッシュ等の光を発するものや三脚、自撮り棒等はご使用にならないでください。

 Please keep luggage and oversized bags in a locker behind the reception on the first floor.
大きな手荷物は1階受付裏のロッカーにお預けください。

 Talking on cellular phones is not permitted.
館内での携帯電話の通話はご遠慮ください。

 Food and drink may not be brought into the museum.
館内での飲食、ガムはご遠慮ください。

 Smoking is prohibited in the museum or on the museum grounds.
館内（敷地内）での喫煙はご遠慮ください。

 Please only use pencils and dry media when writing inside the museum.
展示室内での筆記用具は鉛筆のみご利用いただけます。

 Please refrain from using strollers due to limited space. They can be stored at the reception.
館内のスペースが限られているためベビーカーのご利用はご遠慮ください。受付で一時お預かりいたしますのでお声がけください。

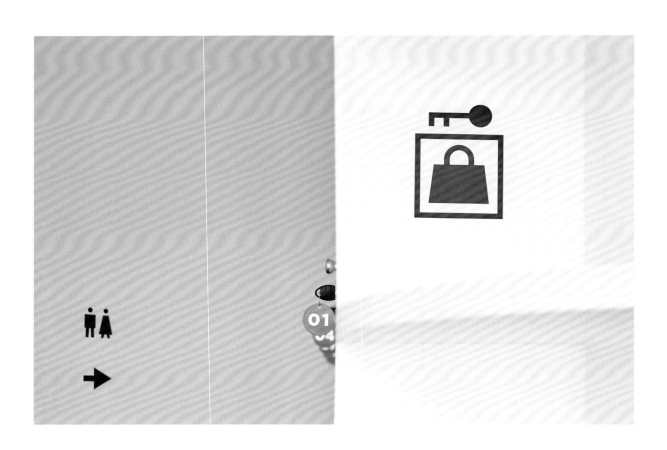

Sukagawa Civic Center tette

Design Agency/ **Irobe Design Institute**
Art Direction/ **Yoshiaki Irobe**
Design/ **Hiroshi Homma, Takumi Adachi**
Client/ **Sukagawa City, Unemori Architects**

This is a signage project for the Sukagawa Civic Center in Sukagawa, Fukushima, a complex built with earthquake restoration assistance funding. The center serves various functions, such as childcare center, lifelong learning spaces, library, event hall and museum. It is an open architectural space without floor-based segmentation. The plan required a design with clear directions and an accessible character for users of all ages.

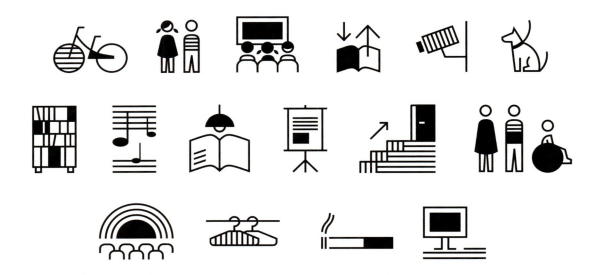

Mediateka in Tychy

Design Agency/ **Blank Studio**
Design/ **Bartlomiej Witanski, Aleksandra Krupa, Weronika Mehr, Adrianna Sowinska**
Photography/ **Barbara Kubska**

Mediateka in Tychy, Poland, is a library for the 21st century. A striking characteristic of this library is that the glass surfaces total almost 4,500 square meters. During this project, Blank Studio was given only a small budget, so the designers decided to use popular materials. Considering the safety of users, the wayfinding design marked almost all glass surfaces with irregular, linear patterns.

Atenció Skater

Design Agency/ **Forma**

Plaça dels Àngels in Barcelona, Spain, is one of the most famous skate plazas in the world. Forma was commissioned to design a campaign to remind skaters to respect the rules of the area. The main goal of this campaign was to set some rules to skate in an iconic spot without disturbing the neighborhood.

Vega Scene

Design Agency/ **Metric**
Photography/ **Thomas Ekström**

This is a wayfinding and visual identity for Oslo's new art-cinema and theater.

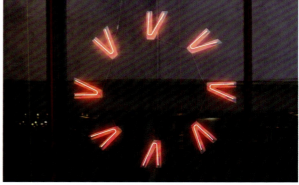

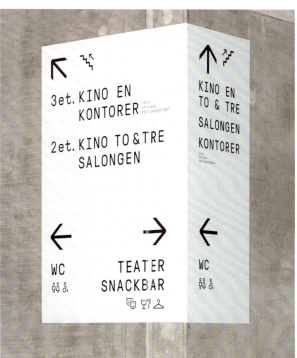
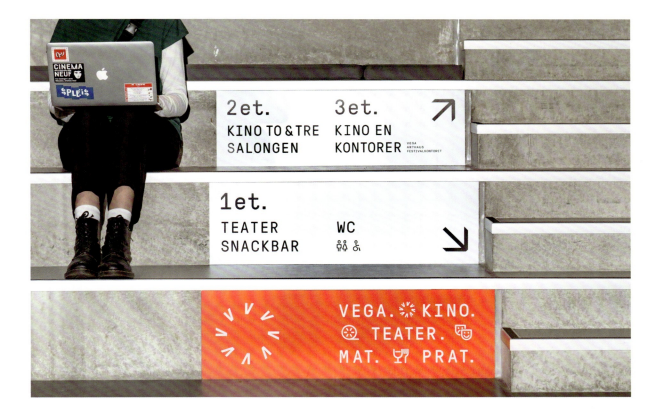

Signage Sports Hall Bitzius

Design Agency/ **Büro Destruct**
Design/ **Lorenz "Lopetz" Gianfreda**
Photography/
Architekturfotografie Gempeler
Client/ **wbarchitekten**

Signage design was needed for the school sports hall, Turnhalle Bitzius, in Bern, Switzerland. According to the requirements of the architect client, wbarchitekten, Lorenz "Lopetz" Gianfreda from Büro Destruct created a clean, simple, but humorous and sporty set of icons for the signage of the building.

Nijinoki Nursery School

Design Agency/ **KARAPPO Inc.**
Client/ **Fujitsu Limited**

Inspired by the name of the nursery school, Nijinoki, which means a rainbow tree, KARAPPO Inc. designed a logo and signage system for it. The signs were installed on the lower part of the wall, which enables children to see them more easily. KARAPPO Inc. also shaped them into plump and round shapes to suit the doors and notice boards, which makes a soft atmosphere.

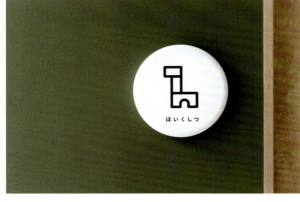 

ZUCZUG Head Office Sign Design

Design Agency/ **702design**

702design was commissioned to design the signage for ZUCZUG. To make it more interesting and playful, 702design made an elegant representation of each feature icon. These funny and humorous graphics make the tense office atmosphere feel more relaxed.

Volksschule Edlach

Design Agency/ **Sägenvier DesignKommunikation**
Design/ **Sigi Ramoser, Barbara Raich, Martin Platzgummer**
Photography/ **Darko Todorovic**

Volksschule Edlach is a wayfinding project for the Primary School of Dornbirn Edlach. The designers used flags as a nexus between classes and their rooms. Enhanced by different emblematic animals, a strong sense of community turns classes into groups of discoverers and reflects their team spirit on the inside and outside. These emblematic animals also created a system, using its contrast to place the children's fantasies in between the outer world and daily school life.

MEDIATEKA
Culture Spot

Design Agency/ **MuchaDSGN**
Art Direction & Design/ **Konrad Moszyński**
Photography/ **Konrad Moszyński**

MEDIATEKA Culture Spot is a modern, fully interactive cultural center. The wayfinding project for this facility was to inform and properly direct all visitors, but also had an aesthetic function, complementing the interior design of the building created by architect Paulina Walkow. The vertical stripes, which decorate the outside of the windows and the inside of the window panes, resemble both a collection of books and piano keys. And the portrait of Krzysztof Komeda, a famous Polish composer, is in one of the icons.

Muzyka
kompozycja
aranżacja
nagrania
instrumenty

Studio Komeda

Szatnia

Simon Wayfinding

Design Agency/ **Forma**

Simon is a manufacturer of small electrical materials in Spain. Forma was commissioned to design new signage for the refurbished headquarters.

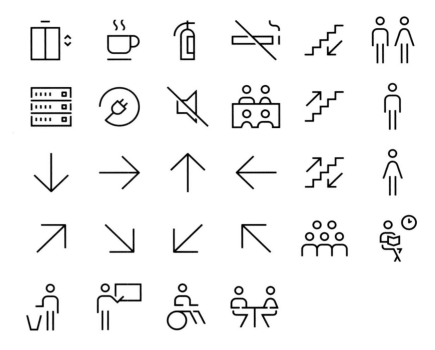

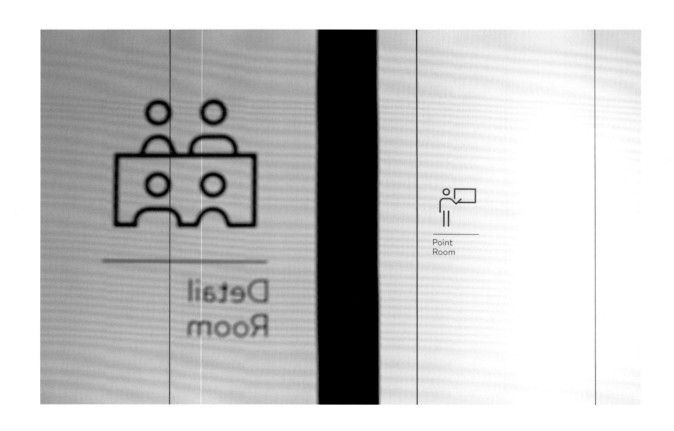

Sala de reuniones
 Tutoría
 Aula
 Biblioteca
Coordinación
Sala de reuniones
Psicología

 Garita
 Cuarto de máquinas
 Laboratorio de física
 Inspección
 Timbre
Baño

Unidad Educativa Particular Marista

Design/ **Mateo Flandoli**
Client/ **Espinoza Carvajal Architects**

Mateo Flandoli was commissioned to design a wayfinding system for the Marist School. In collaboration with the architects, they defined the nomenclature for the blocks, classrooms, administrative and functional spaces. The information was synthesized in a system organized by icons, colors and typography that were integrated into the architecture achieving different levels of communication with directional, identifying and decorative signs.

Madison Shopping Center

Design Agency/ **UVMW**
Creative & Art Direction/ **Robert Mendel, Jacek Walesiak**
Design/ **Robert Mendel, Jacek Walesiak, Michał Małolepszy, Marta Czuban**
Photography/ **Rafał Kołsut**

Madison Shopping Center is a small building located next to the old town of Gdańsk, Poland. The foundation of this project was to point out the city's features in the Madison Shopping Center's various structures and activity areas. The logo and the authorial modular grid became a flexible tool for creating compelling advertising and image compositions.

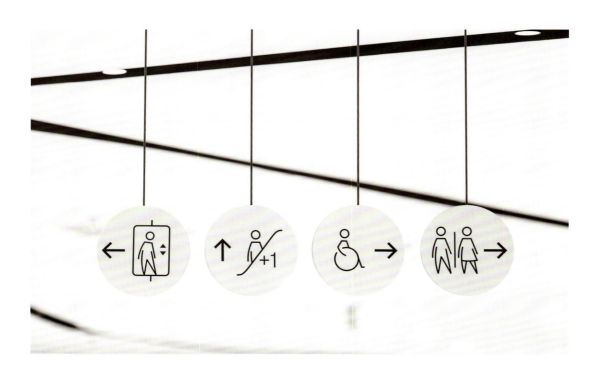

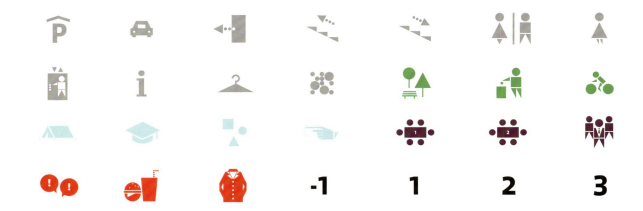

NInA

Design Agency/ **UVMW**
Creative & Art Direction/ **Robert Mendel, Jacek Walesiak**
Design/ **Robert Mendel, Jacek Walesiak, Marta Czuban**
Photography/ **Aleksandra Pavoni**

National Audiovisual Institute (NInA) is a wayfinding project. The designers were asked to design a wayfinding system for the new headquarters of NInA in Poland. The four stories were differentiated by using different colors. The graphic elements were elaborated based on NInA's new logotype. All carriers, pictograms and messages were created with a dynamic information system that can be changed, if necessary.

National Stadium in Warsaw

Design Agency/ **UVMW**
Creative & Art Direction/ **Robert Mendel, Jacek Walesiak**
Design/ **Robert Mendel, Jacek Walesiak, Piotr Matejkowski, Małgorzata Masłowska**
Photography/ **Mateusz Kawęczyński, Robert Mendel**

The existing wayfinding system of the Polish National Stadium is lacking some information. The designers were commissioned to redesign the system and add the missing information. They chose red and white as the basic colors for the system in reference to the color of the building and embedded them into the building's identity. For the particular zones, there is a color coding system, which leads the audience from outer parking lots to their seats.

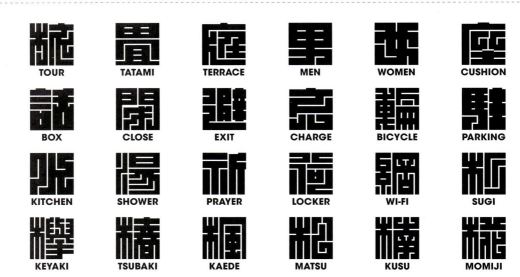

Inbound League

Design Agency/ **SKG**
Art Direction/ **Makoto Sukegawa**
Design/ **Makoto Sukegawa, Ikuko Tokumo**
Client/ **UDS**
Photography/ **Kohei Yamamoto**

SKG designed the logo for the Inbound League, a place for people who take part in global and local business. In consideration of foreign users, the symbol mark was designed using the motif of Genjikō no zu, known as a kumikō (an incense-comparing game) describing The Tale of Genji. Also, SKG used the Kakuji, one kind of Edomoji, as inspiration for the sign's design. By adding English to the Kakuji, SKG thought it would be easier to experience the Japanese culture of kanji and provide a new opportunity for communication.

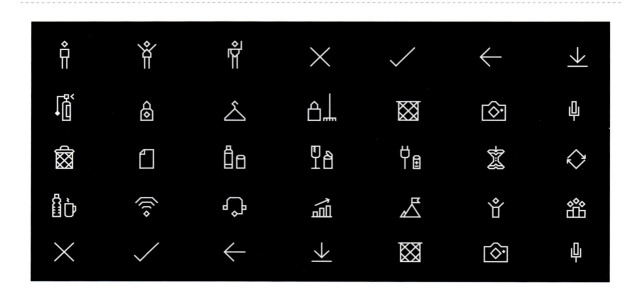

Fremtind

Design Agency/ **Scandinavian Design Group**
Design/ **Bendik Ramm, Nicklas Haslestad**
Type Design/ **Robin Mientjes**

Fremtind is a life insurance company for the future, focusing on digital innovation—rooted in customer insights and needs. Scandinavian Design Group's concept builds on the associations within the name. "Frem" means forward and "tind" means pinnacle. The typographic system ensures a clear and transparent design on all surfaces, making the identity simple to work with and understandable for all audiences. The entire identity system is based on the principle of clarity. To top it off, the image gallery adds warmth, love and safety, supporting Fremtind's need to be present in the most intimate times in their customers' lives.

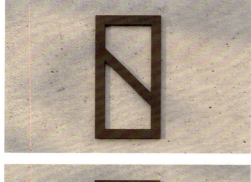

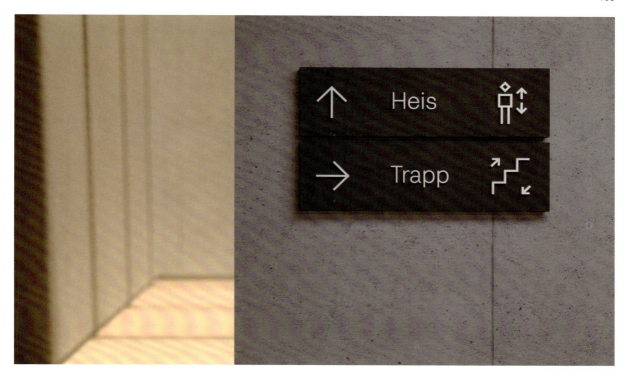

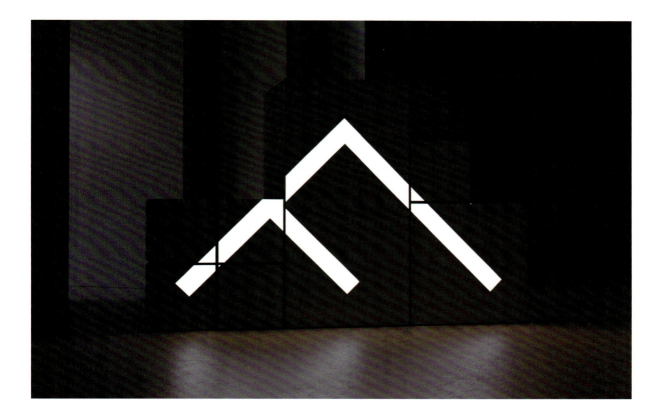

S5

Design Agency/ **Metric**
Photography/ **Thomas Ekström**

This is a wayfinding and visual identity for S5, an office building in Fredrikstad, Norway.

Sentralen

Design Agency/ **Metric**
Photography/ **Thomas Ekström**

This is a wayfinding system and environmental design for Sentralen in Oslo, Norway.

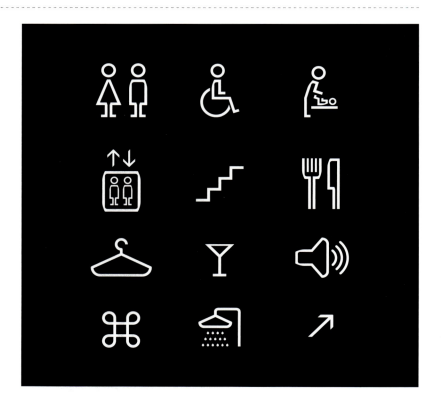

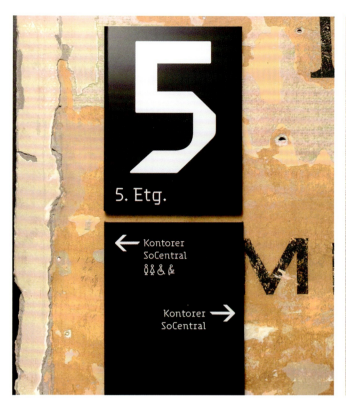

Airport Iconography Proposal

Design/ **Alejandra Melo Plaza**

The creation of this icon family for the new airport in Mexico City was inspired by typeface Rubik. Designed by Hurbert and Fischer, this typeface was inspired by the Rubik's Cube's rounded edges. Based on this, Rubik was selected as a base to bring this icon set to live. Considering the needs of an international airport, 55 icons were created to fulfill different functions such as presenting services and amenities for passengers at the new airport.

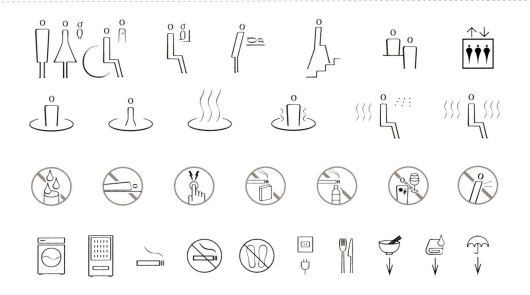

Vessel Hotel Campana Susukino

Design Agency/ **SKG**
Creeative Direction/ **UDS**
Client/ **Vessel Hotel Development Co., Ltd.**

Based on the concept of interior design, SKG designed the signage with elements of brushstrokes and traditional Ainu patterns, which are essential to the Japanese impression. SKG created an original typeface for the hotel, which it used to display room numbers and signage in the halls.

Museum of Józef Piłsudski in Sulejówek

Design Agency/ **Kolektyf**
Design/ **Katarzyna Cimała, Alicja Chojnacka, Marta Przeciszewska, Magdalena Szwajcowska, Bartosz Zieliński**
Photography/ **Filip Basara**

This museum is located on the first marshal of Poland Józef Piłsudski's former property in Sulejówek. It consists of the historical buildings and a new facility made of concrete. Kolektyf designed a signage system in the museum. They came up with signboards using inner walls and a set of icons, inspired by the Konkret Grotesk Font, with subtle colors and graphics relating to the museum's brand book.

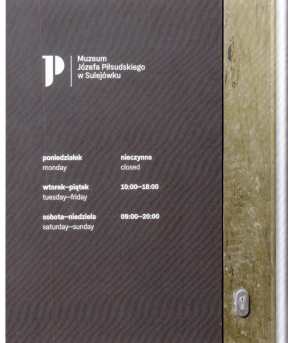

Nowy Targ Office Building in Wrocław

Design Agency/ **Kolektyf**
Design/ **Katarzyna Cimała, Marta Przeciszewska, Magdalena Szwajcowska, Bartek Zieliński**
Photography/ **Karolina Kosowicz**

Kolektyf designed a signage system for the office building Nowy Targ in Wrocław, Poland. The building stands out with its concrete finish. The building's architecture inspired the designers to limit the means of expression and apply minimalism in the design. In terms of graphics, they chose large, stylish typography and solid, decisive cuts. The stylish signage was consistently applied throughout the building—from the underground garage to office space with different materials used depending on the function of the space.

Medic-r

Design Agency/ **Uniforma**
Interior Design/ **Biuro Struktura**

Medic-r is a clinic in the heart of Jeżyce in Poznań, Poland. The goal was to design a visual identity of a clinic that was supposed to be perceived more like a spa than a treatment facility. Uniforma designed the complete branding, collaterals, a new website and an interior wayfinding system. Uniforma thought Medic-r is a great example of how graphic design can work together with architecture and be an important part of the whole experience.

Saint-Paul Hostel

Design/ **Stéphanie Aubin**
Client/ **Saint-Paul Hostel**
Photography/ **Katya Konioukhova**

Saint-Paul Hostel is located in the old port area of Montreal, Canada. This youth hostel is a vibrant center of life, welcoming travelers from around the world. Stéphanie Aubin wished to express that feeling of movement within the logo and signage design. She explored a modern style for the icon design. Thick lines, geometry and simplicity are perfect words to describe the style of the signage icons.

Container Hotel

Design Agency/ **LIE**
Art Direction & Design/ **Driv Loo**
Interior Design/ **Tetawowe**
Client/ **Container Hotel**

The Container Hotel was built from renewable-freight-containers, bringing the value and concept of sustainability and practicality. Inspired by the graphics on shipping containers, the designers created a bold and modern identity with a full visual language based on the same grid system.

Casa Museo Wayfinding ID

Design/ **Atemporal Agency, Hermes Mazali, Luis Fasah**
Icon Design/ **Hermes Mazali**
Wayfinding Design/ **Luis Fasah, Hermes Mazali**

This project is based on the house-museum dedicated to the former first lady of Argentina, Eva Peron, in the city of Buenos Aires. The designers created a visual and signage identity for the space. Hermes Mazali worked on the synthesis of the tri-band Argentinian flag. With the three parallel bands, he designed the rest of the icons to establish a simple, but particular style.

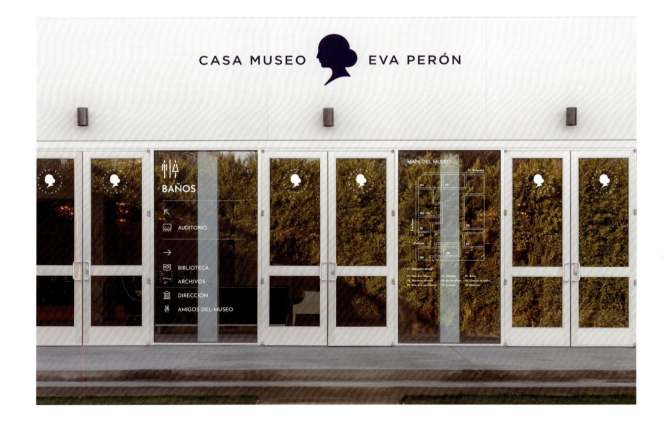

S/PARK

Art Direction & Creative Direction/
Masaki Hanahara
Executive Creative Direction/
Yoji Nobuto
Design/ **Ikki Kobayashi**

S/PARK is a new, beautiful complex built for the Japanese beauty company SHISEIDO. The designers first focused on SHISEIDO's exclusive typeface that had been used for advertising and packaging for over 100 years. Then, the designers created a new font and logos using components of the Japanese word "bi," which means beauty. They wanted to create a design that conveys Japanese-ness to global consumers by using SHISEIDO's typeface, one of the company's historical assets. It was challenging to make the design look modern, rather than old-fashioned while preserving the essence of the original typeface.

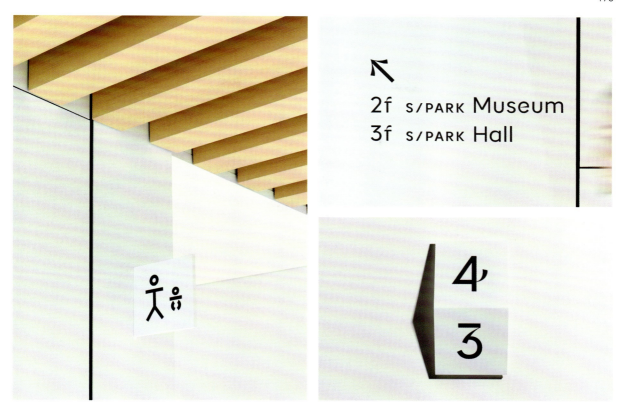

La Casa Encendida

Design Agency/ **POINT OF REFERENCE Studio**
Art Direction/ **Jeffrey Ludlow**
Design/ **Jeffrey Ludlow, Anabel Maldonado**

La Casa Encendida is a Madrid, Spain-based social and cultural center, located in a restored building. POR Studio's task was to design a neutral signage system that re-emphasizes the architecture and is accessible to all visitors. The pictograms were based on the building, and they communicate the diverse programs within the center. Overall, the signage system is recognized as one of the most accessible and clear systems in Spain.

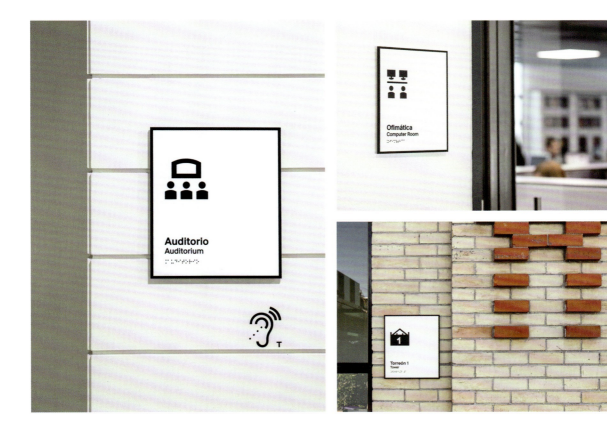

BUSS by Allianz

Design Agency/ **Nusae**
Art Direction/ **Andi Rahmat**
Design/ **Darindra Suraji**

BUSS is an official business partner of Allianz Life Indonesia. For its newest office space and café, BUSS required a modern design approach to create a relaxing ambiance. The pictogram is characterized by dynamic pen-like strokes to communicate its concept further. The signage is formed by galvanized frames and acrylic. The opening graphic ambiance is a translation from the client's core concept. The graphics are implemented in incomplete forms that complete each other, creating readable letters.

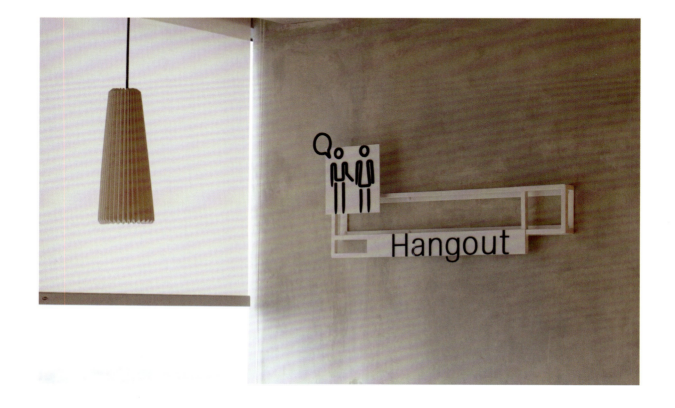

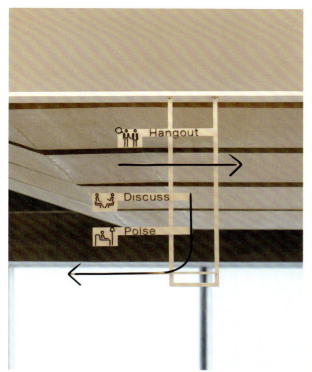

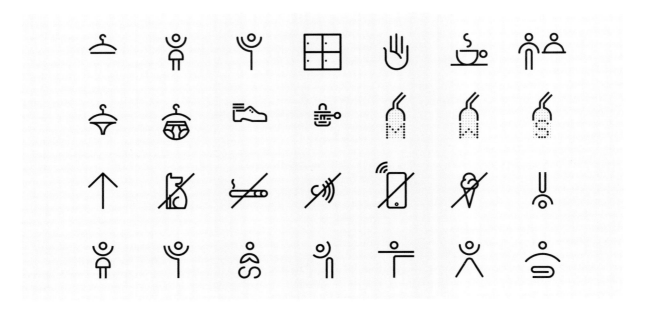

Hot Yo Studio

Design Agency/ **Nusae**
Art Direction/ **Andi Rahmat**
Design/ **Lutfi Aziz**

Hot Yo Studio is a yoga studio based in Kuala Lumpur, Malaysia. Nusae opted to develop amusing pictograms that perfectly represent wellness through clear and simple design. While pictograms are typically functional, here, the designers gave them a decorative meaning. All the communicative matters were characterized through the use of customized typography, which was developed as a hybrid of yoga poses and alphabetical expression.

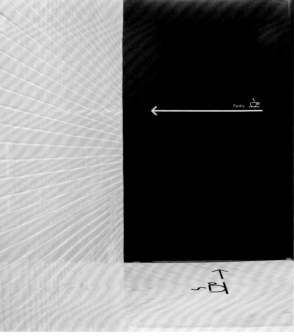

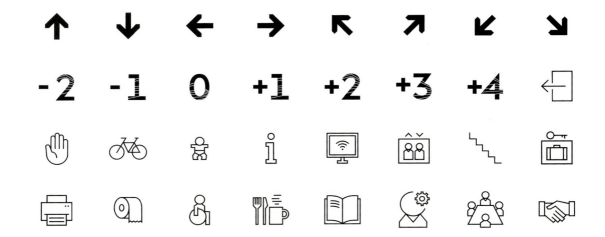

De Krook

Design Agency/ **DIFT**
Art Direction/ **Fien Meelberghs, Yves Drieghe**
Client/ **De Krook Library**
Photography/ **DIFT**

De Krook is an architectural gem in Ghent, Belgium, that houses the city library, several research labs and much more. DIFT's goal was to create a pleasant customer journey and to give a warm welcome to every visitor. To create a functional overview, DIFT took the floor levels as the most important point of orientation. The destination type served as the second layer. Five recognizable icons represent the five central functions of De Krook, making it easy to find the way to the library or café. Finally, DIFT designed tailor-made practical pictograms for all direction indicators and utilities.

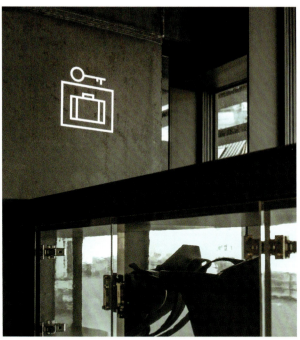

Signage for Augusta Raurica

Design Agency/ **SUAN Conceptual Design**
Art Direction/ **Esther Stute**
Creative Direction/ **Susanne Hartmann, André Konrad**
Client/ **Augusta Raurica**

Augusta Raurica Roman Museum asked SUAN to redesign the entrance area. To improve the orientation of the visitors, SUAN was commissioned to design a new signage system and the corresponding inscriptions. The concept was based on a new icon grid that builds on the components of the logo and thus blends in harmoniously with the existing design elements of Augusta Raurica. With clear and graphic language, the signage system creates a balanced contrast to the ancient Roman remains.

Adana Archaeology Museum Wayfinding Design

There was no wayfinding design in Adana Archaeology Museum in Adana, Turkey, so İrem Uyar designed a system inspired by old-style patterns. She used black, white, gray and red colors to create a contrast with the dark interior of the museum.

Art Direction & Design/ **İrem Uyar**
Photography/ **İrem Uyar**

The University Children's Hospital of Kraków

Design/ **Zuzanna Opozda**

The information system of this project consists of external and internal signage: collective, directional and places' signage. Zuzanna Opozda proposed her division of units and the simplification of the names of buildings. Logo redesign preserves the symbolism of the old sign—children and the sun. She combined this symbolism with a simple drawing of pictograms to create consistent branding, easily translatable to various media.

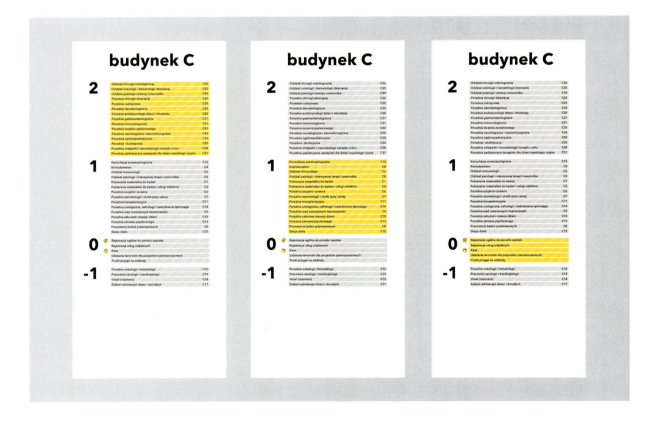

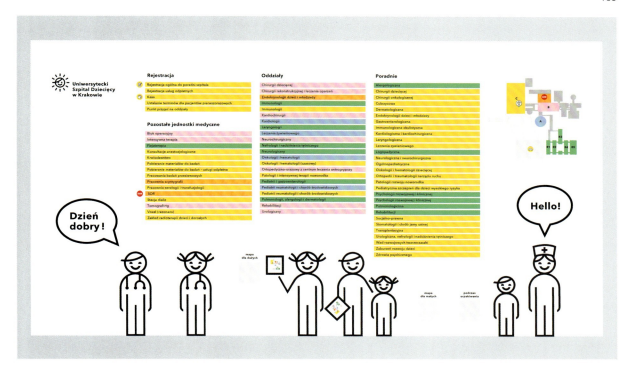

New's To-O

Design Agency/ **Arata Takemoto Design**
Client/ **The To-O Nippo Press Co., Ltd.**
Photography/ **Tomooki Kengaku**

Arata Takemoto Design designed a new wayfinding system for the cultural complex New's To-O. Arata Takemoto Design extracted the elements of kokeshi, a Japanese wooden doll without limbs but with a spherical head and a cylindrical body, to create an organic design with a relaxed appearance.

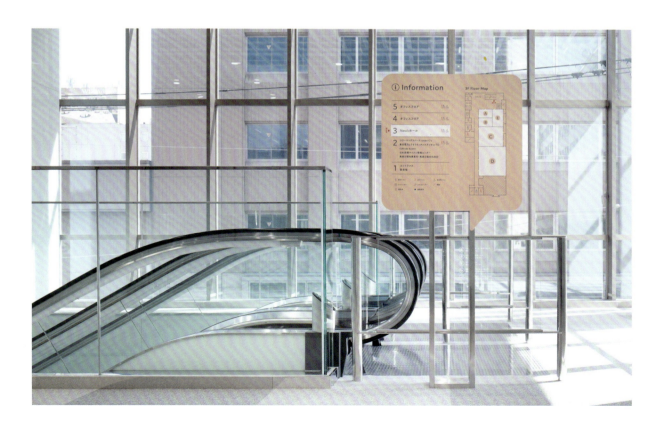

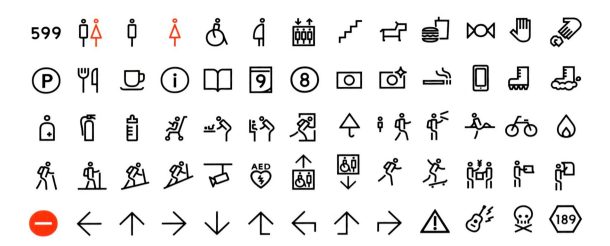

Takao 599 Museum

Design Agency/ **Daikoku Design Institute**
Art & Creative Direction/ **Daigo Daikoku**
Design/ **Daigo Daikoku, Mayumi Sano, Yuto Kanke, Naoko Sasaki, Hana Yazaki**
Photography/ **Taiji Yamazaki**

Takao 599 Museum is a museum for Mount Takao, which stands 599 meters tall at the edge of Tokyo. Despite its low elevation, Mount Takao is the world's most visited mountain, and this museum aims to convey its allure to visitors from all over the world. The pictogram system for Takao affords smooth scalability and affinity for motion, allowing itself to translate well across all media. It is used throughout the museum on a variety of dynamic and static media, aiding the museum to maintain instinctive and informative communication with its visitors.

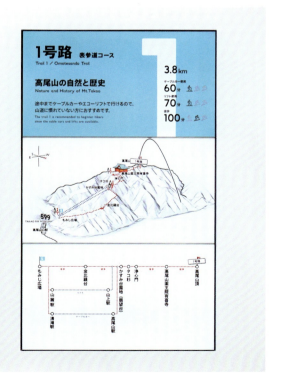

The Feluma Theater

Design Agency/ **Greco Design**
Design/ **Gustavo Greco, Tidé Soares, Emília Junqueira, Paula Sallum, Alexandre Fonseca**
Photography/ **Rafael Motta**

The Feluma Theater is a performance hall that was inaugurated in December 2019 in Belo Horizonte, Brazil. This signage system displays the function of the light that it projects through the equipment when focusing on an object on the stage. The yellow paint on the wall and black acrylic touches highlight the information like a scene element. The symbols, arrows and pictograms were imitated from the features of the typeface chosen for the brand—FF Absara Pro.

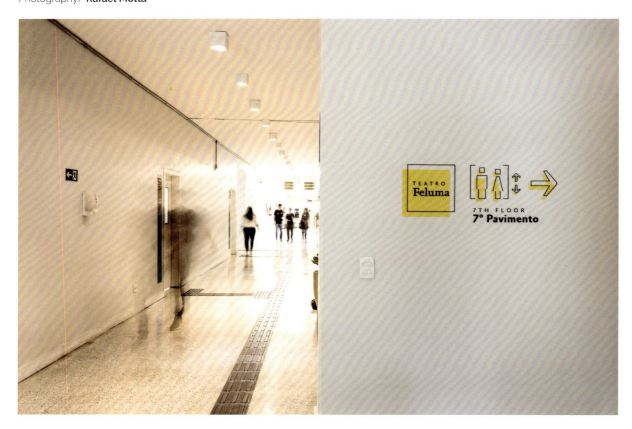

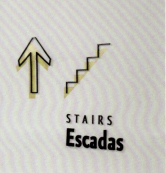

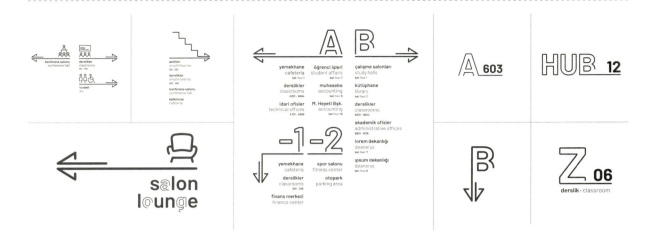

Istanbul Kultur University

Design Agency/ **POMPAA**
Art Direction/ **Ferhat Büyükdağ**
Creative Direction/ **Petek Kızılelma**
Client/ **Istanbul Kultur University**

POMPAA designed the wayfinding system and interior graphics for the new complex of Istanbul Kultur University. The complex is composed of two separate buildings connected from two underground levels. They aimed to create an effective and easy orientation within the complex and design a visual language that will attract its audience. Rather than placing extra units in the building, they tried to use existing surfaces effectively. A visual language was set by using large icons, arrows and colorful surfaces.

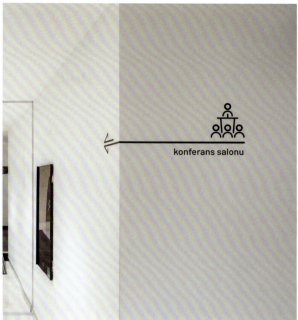

The Software House Office

Design Agency/ **Blank Studio**
Design/ **Bartlomiej Witanski, Aleksandra Krupa, Martyna Berger, Justyna Batko**

This project was based on simplicity, fun and utility. The pictogram system Blank Studio designed is consistent with the interior designers' vision and the toned-down and pleasant style of the interiors. It is also linked to the friendly atmosphere that the company creates for its employees—it provokes play and togetherness. They managed to design a set of unique icons for the rooms and employees can switch their names, such as koteł (cat), okneł (window) and iluminateł (illuminati).

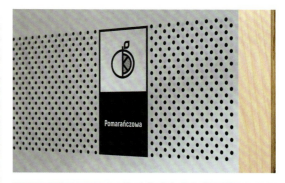

Santander

Design Agency/ **Inplace**
Photography/ **Inplace**

Inplace designed the environmental graphics and wayfinding system for Santander. They accurately and directly represented the main attributes of Santander—simplicity, individuality and fairness. When designing the wayfinding system, they focused on icons' structure and the integration of the font TT Norms in the whole project.

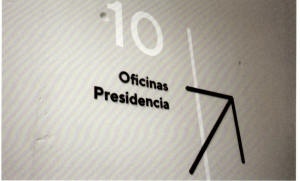

Kimitsu City School Lunch Cooking Facility

Design Agency/ **ujidesign**
Client/ **Kimitsu City**

This project was for a school lunch supply center in Kimitsu, Japan. The students from the neighboring schools visit there as an educational trip. The illustrations about school lunches were displayed everywhere, so that the students can learn about lunches in a fun way. Also, ujidesign arranged the letters such as "煮 (cook)" and "洗 (wash)" distinctively for students and staff to easily recognize different cooking processes.

17th FINA World Championships Budapest

Design Agency/
Graphasel Design Studio

The FINA World Championships are the world championships for aquatic sports, including swimming, diving, high diving, open water swimming, artistic swimming and water polo. In addition to designing the graphic environment and more than 80 pictograms, designing the user experience itself was the greatest work. When constructing the icons, the design team adopted the principles of the logo, but modifed it slightly, then created a much more structured system. By fixing the tilted angles of the lines, adjusting the curves and the distances between the lines, they could address varied needs during the competition.

INTERACTIVE DESIGN

On the Internet nowadays, most websites and apps use icons. They are an essential part of many interactions, directly expressing objects, actions and ideas. In this chapter, we will see how icons benefit interactive design.

TRANSPORTATION

Camping
Design/ **Smalllike**

Transportation Icon Set
Design/ **Monkik**

INTERNET AND TECHNOLOGY

Smart Home

Design/ **Kerismaker Studio**

Smart Technology Malibu Volume 1

Design/ **flat-icons.com**

COMMODITY

On the Way

Design/ **Elisabetta Calabritto**

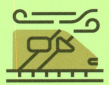   

Pack it Up

Design/ **Elisabetta Calabritto**

FOOD

Underwater
Design/ **Elisabetta Calabritto**

Fast Food Icon Set
Design/ **Dmitriy Mirolyubov**

LANDMARKS

World Landmark Icon Set

Design/ **Microdot Graphic**

MEDICAL

Medical & Healthcare Vol.1

Design/ **Microdot Graphic**

Medical Center

Design/ **Kerismaker Studio**

BUSINESS

Business & Finance Icon Set

Design/ **Microdot Graphic**

Project Management

Design/ **Kerismaker Studio**

Interview with
Tom Birch

Q: Would you like to share some stories about graphic design? How did you get started as a graphic designer?

A: I didn't take a traditional path. I originally studied fine art. However, after graduation, I wanted to create works that can communicate with more people outside of the gallery walls. I feel art education is invaluable. It has taught me to place a concept in the heart of a project. In essence, when making art, you have to communicate complex ideas visually and immediately. Personally, the same is true for design. I don't believe that a degree is the only stepping stone to the design industry. At least, no one has once asked to see mine.

Q: Icons play an important role in many UI/UX designs. They can visually express ideas, objects and actions. Despite these advantages, icons can cause usability problems when designers hide functionality behind icons that are difficult to identify. What do you think of this phenomenon?

A: Icons are symbols and a visual shorthand. Think of the omnipresent "hamburger icon." Its meaning isn't intuitive, but it has become part of our shared vocabulary and, for now at least, it holds as much meaning as the word "menu." In terms of "system icons," it's now an accepted standard to include a descriptive label. Perhaps controversially, I would prefer the singular interruption of having to learn an icon's meaning once, as opposed to repeated interruptions when navigating a visually cluttered UI. I feel the routing problem is often in the app's architecture as opposed to focusing on an individual element. Therefore, simplicity is often the key.

Q: Your project Re·view carries a style of editorial illustration. How did you come up with such an idea?

A: Re·view offers commentary on the news and media. The visual style references the language of newsprint, incorporating heavy serif fonts, editorial illustrations and halftone patterns.

Throughout the app, icons are used more like illustrated pictograms in an attempt to help explain abstract concepts. For this reason, they don't have to follow the conventions of traditional interface or "system icons," such as being identifiable at small sizes or as readily self-evident.

Q: In recent years, you have designed several apps. The icon became an essential part of screen design. What do you think are the key attributes of the icon on the app's interface?

A: Icons are another touchpoint of a brand and should feel aligned to the larger identity. I've worked on a number of apps and found that there is a tendency for the digital product to become something separated from its brand. This may increase the ubiquity in the design. Sometimes I look at my phone and forget which app I'm using. However, in general, there are technical limitations that dictate some design choices, like target sizes, reachability and accessibility guidelines. Icons predate screens. Our relationship with technology is constantly evolving. The way we interact with our devices today certainly won't be the same in the future. However, icons will always have their place in communication.

Q: What do you do before designing icons for an app?

A: Icons should be designed in consideration of the audience. What seems obvious to the designer might not translate to all people and for that reason, it's important to think beyond one's own immediate culture and references. I tend to start by writing a list of synonyms to abstract the theme and help find a relatable metaphor. Working on Re·view, I found humor was a useful tool in translating an icon's meaning and avoiding clichés.

Re·view App

Design/ **Tom Birch**

Re·view is an app that aims to highlight the bias and misdirection of the press. To help the user connect with new terminology, an extensive glossary is explained by a suite of 30 memorable pictograms. This design asks people to question and engage with social issues, equipping them with tools to detect faulty reasoning. The half-tone patterns and headline serifs reference the aesthetics of print newspapers to distinguish themselves from the expected digital trends.

Behance

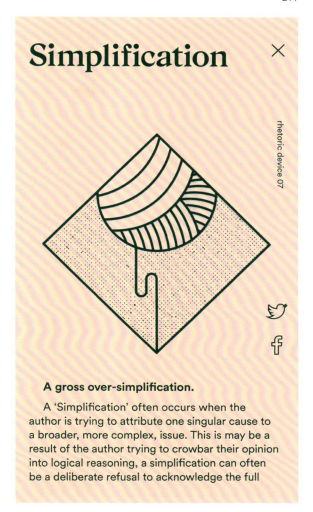

Q: Graphic design is different from fine art. By following the requirements of customers, the designed works may tend to be commercial. How do you balance creativity and the demands of your clients?

A: I believe that the most interesting design is made in partnership with the clients. Sometimes it can be a challenging process, but collaboration is the best way to uncover and distill the essence of a brand. In my experience, graphic design is more than pure aesthetics. Instead, work is rooted in insight and strategy from the outset. It's from here that I find the real opportunities for creativity. Each designer and studio will have their own process and set of values and it can be difficult to balance these with every client. It is important to remember that not all clients are a good match for you.

Q: You have been involved in different areas of design like brand identities, apps, album artworks and so on. What's your plan in the field of design?

A: My main interest is branding. I believe it's the combination of design and culture that creates more meaningful work that speaks to people. I'm currently working in a design agency. I really like working with different people and the collaboration that offers—it's a great place to bounce around ideas and create something that wouldn't have been possible alone. If I look into the future, I would like to create works that connect with more people outside of the design community and have a positive impact on the world.

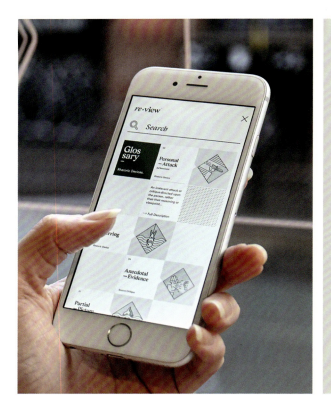
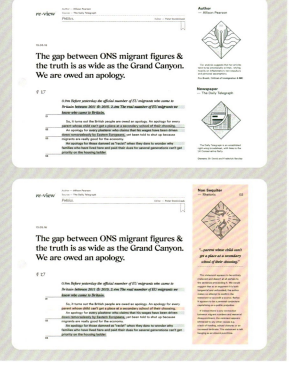

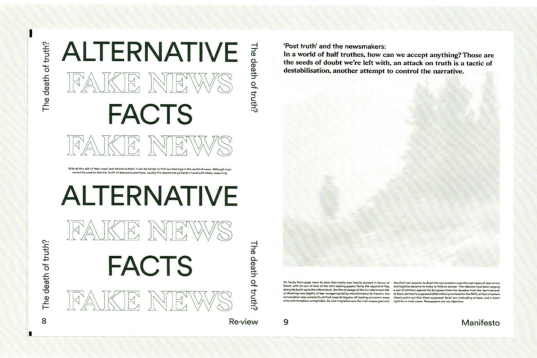

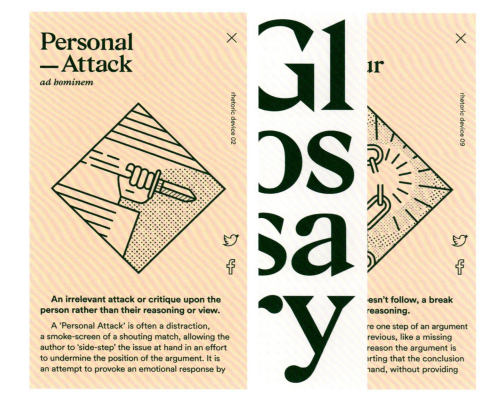

eat to be_

Design Agency/ **The Woork Co**

eat to be_ is a mobile app that serves as a tool for nutrition-related coaches and influencers. The Woork Co created the name "eat to be_" for the app. The logotype was set with bites on *a* and *b* and an underscore "_" which invites users to complete the phrase with a word or an icon, closer to an emoji and visual chat world. To complete the brand, The Woork Co also created bold thick stroke icons and chose a warm, food-related color combination.

Official

Behance

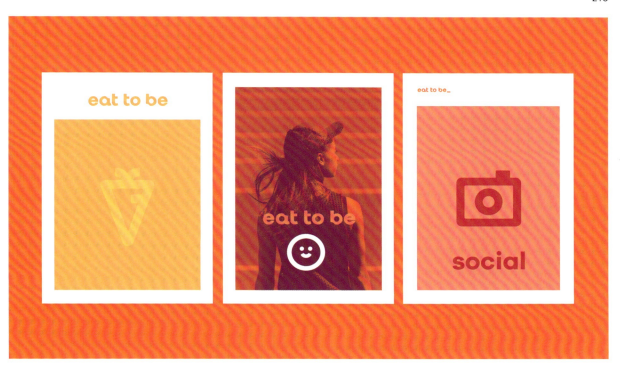
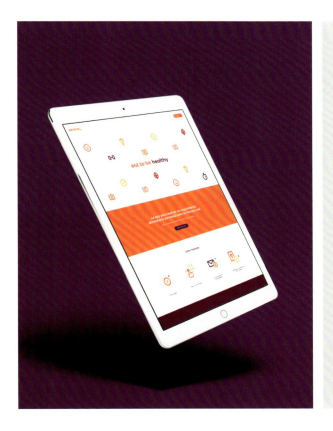

Connected

Design Agency/ **Underline Studio**
Creative Direction/ **Fidel Peña, Claire Dawson**
Illustration/ **Christopher DeLorenzo**
Design/ **Cameron McKague, Fidel Peña**
Client/ **Connected**

Connected is a software development company composed of strategists, designers and engineers. Obsessed with powerful user experiences and technologies, Connected believes they can fulfill their single passion—to build better products. Underline Studio designed the new logo and identity for the brand that represents who Connected is today.

Official

Behance

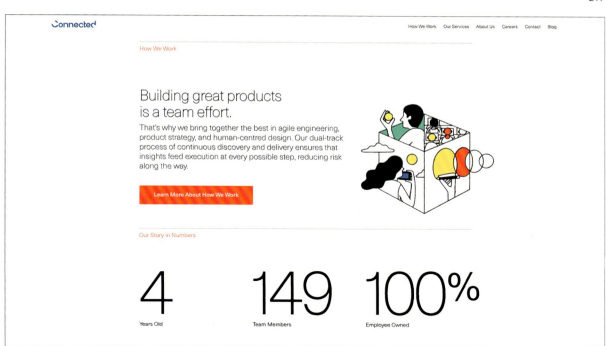

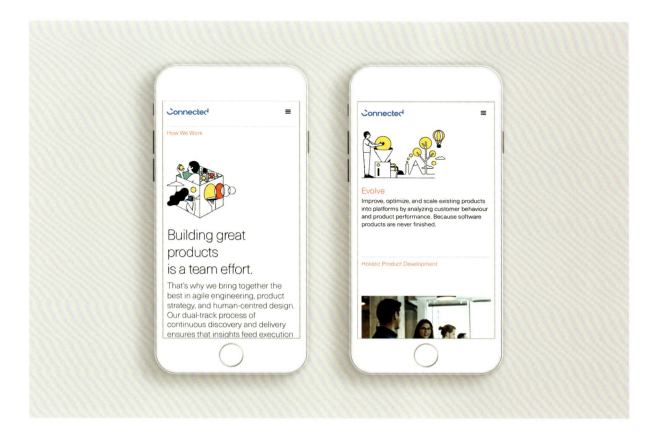

The Darwin Challenge

Design Agency/ **Universal Favourite**
Creative Direction/ **Dari Israelstam**
Illustration/ **Janine Rewell**
Design/ **Bonnie Nguyen**
Client/ **The Darwin Challenge**

Universal Favourite was commissioned to create an app to raise people's awareness of preventing the global mass extinction of species by eating less meat. The app has been at the epicenter of the birth of a movement that has brought together many organizations, groups and individuals, and as that community engages and grows, the influence and impact spread.

Official

App Store

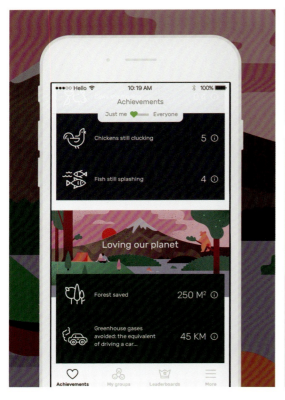
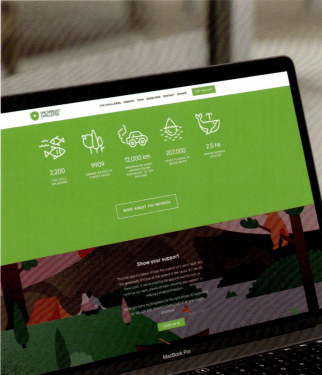

Good Pair Days

Design Agency/ **Universal Favourite**
Creative Direction/ **Dari Israelstam**
Design/ **Meghan Armstrong, Bonnie Nguyen**
Client/ **Good Pair Days**
Styling/ **Jessica Johnson**
Photography/ **Benito Martin**

Proclaimed "the Netflix of Wine" by Vogue, the growing start-up, Good Pair Days, pairs customers with the perfect wines for their palates, making them the most advanced wine retailer in the market. Universal Favourite was commissioned to create a visual identity that effectively represents the brand's digital nature without losing the human touch of their exceptional customer service and product experience.

Official

Google Play

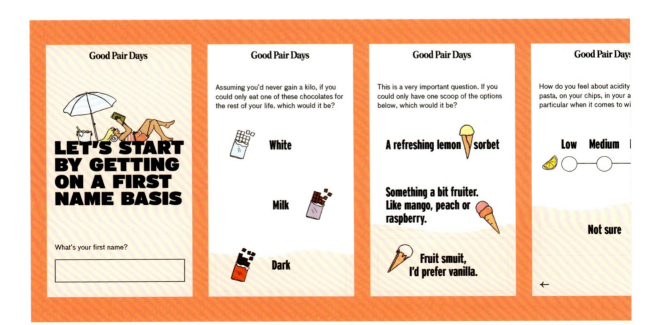

Pro-Aktiv

Design Agency/ **Makers Company**

Pro-Aktiv is a self-initiated project. Makers Company wanted to explore how branding extends to an illustration system for an app. The designers from Makers Company thought the best way to accomplish that was by creating their fictional fitness app and experimenting with a bold character illustration style that fits the theme of exercise. The aim was to create a fun and energetic series of visuals to explain the main features of the app.

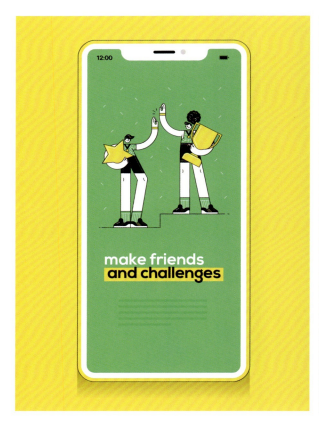

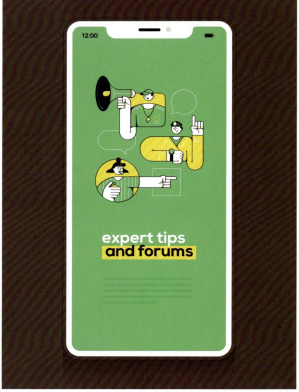

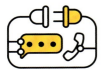

Callibri

Design / **Savelii Shirokov**

Callibri is a marketing boost service that includes two main products: call tracking and online chat. As a part of Callibri's marketing department, Savelii Shirokov was responsible for the task of website redesign and rebranding. It was important to create an easy and understandable visual language that was fun and interesting despite the complexity of the product.

Official

Behance

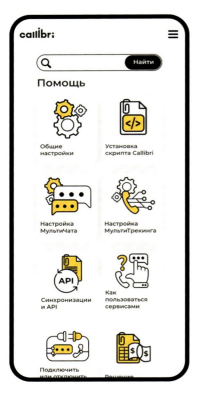  

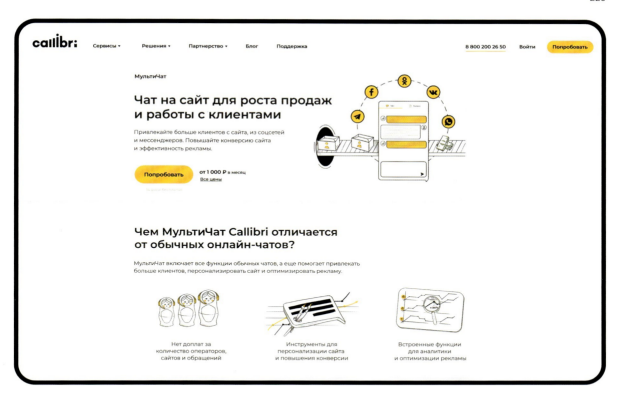

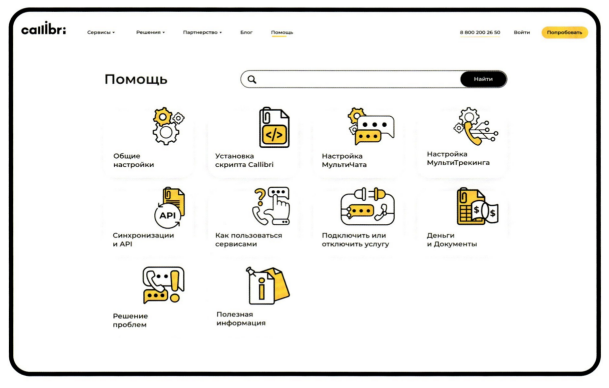

Bankin iOS App Design

Design/ **Ruitong Zhu**

Bankin is an e-wallet app aimed at making personal financial management easier and faster. The icons were designed to convey information and guide users to enjoy each function. The icons are clear and linear, which simplify the complexity of finance itself and improves the visual identity of the brand.

  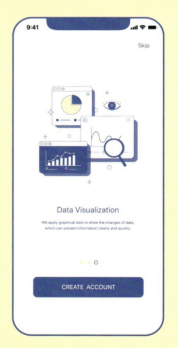

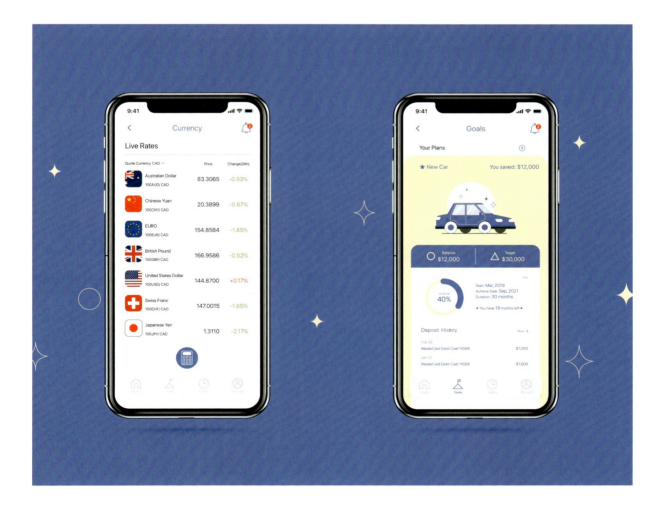

Servo Delivery— Laundry App

Design Agency/ **Assembly Studio**
App & Website Design/ **Appstage**
Copywriting/ **Melissa Buys-Brouard**
Client/ **Dane Harris**

Servo Delivery is a laundry app developed by South African entrepreneur Dane Harris. Assembly Studio was commissioned to design a brand identity for it. Looking to create a brand that could stand out in the digital landscape and appeal to a younger target market, Assembly Studio designed a simple, modern and distinctive brand mark paired with a bold color palette, simple icons and whimsical illustrations for the app.

Behance

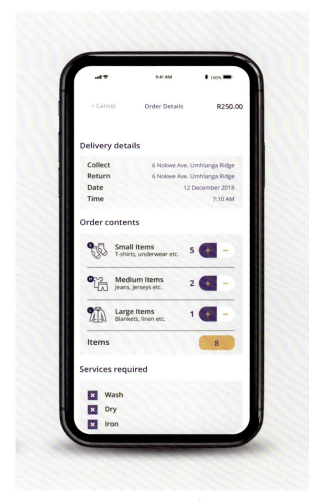

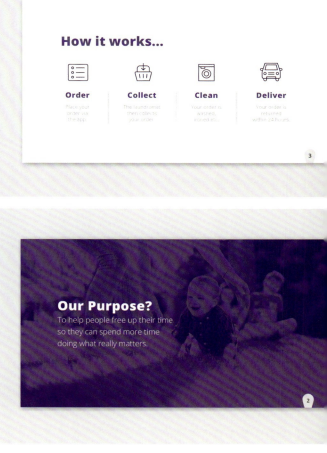

RIDE M.E
—Movable Enjoyment

Design/ **Jihee Kim, Jiyou Park**

RIDE M.E, a service that allows people to enjoy self-driving cars. The design of the RIDE M.E was inspired by self-driving cars with a focus on a futuristic feeling and a new dimension of the driving experience. Based on trusting transportation and new technology, Jihee Kim and Jiyou Park tried to express RIDE M.E as an intuitive and minimal design system. The overall design was carried out by imagining a world in which self-driving cars will be commercialized in the future.

Behance

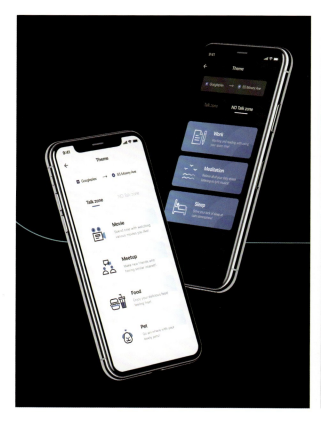

BeeBetter—Habit Tracker App

Design/ **Anastasiia Mysliuk**

People often try to develop new and good habits. But most of them stop trying after the first week and only a few manage to make a useful habit part of their daily routine. This app makes the process of making habits fun and interactive, engages friends' support for additional motivation and shows the user ongoing progress.

Behance

  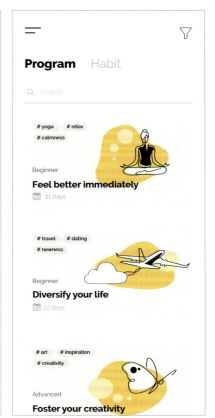

WATERFLOW

Design/ **Victor Gorovoy**

WATERFLOW is a simple iOS app that gives an opportunity to quickly order any amount of water at any place.

Behance

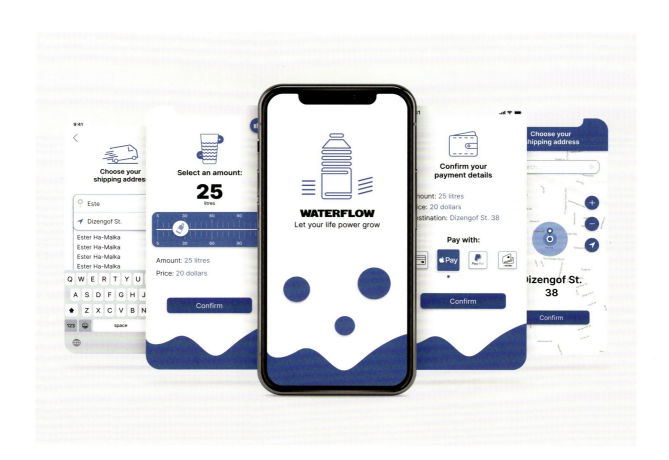

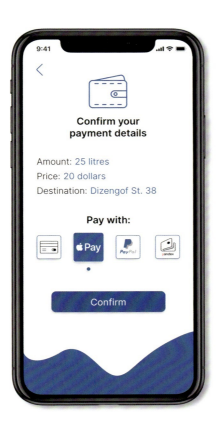
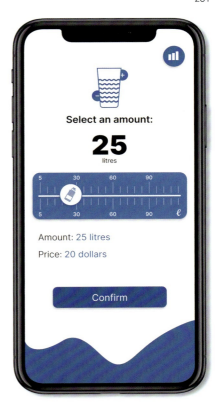
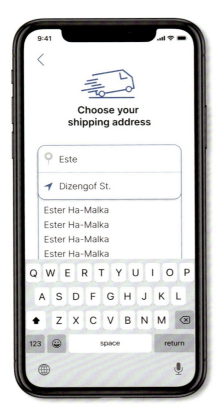

TucomunidApp

Design Agency/ **Bwow Studio**

TucomunidApp is a project based on the need for neighborhood communities. Through the app, the user can vote on decisions, reserve common spaces and report any incident. Bwow Studio designed the web and app to facilitate all management and provide comfort to users.

Behance

Kakao Corp

Creative Direction/ **Seungtae Kim, Minho Kim**
Illustration/ **Joohee Hwang**
Design/ **Seungtae Kim, Jeongeun Yoon, Jieun Huh**

These are the icons used on a company's recruitment website. The site tells the story of Kakao Krew and provides recruiting information. The icons were designed to make the website more friendly and relaxed.

Behance

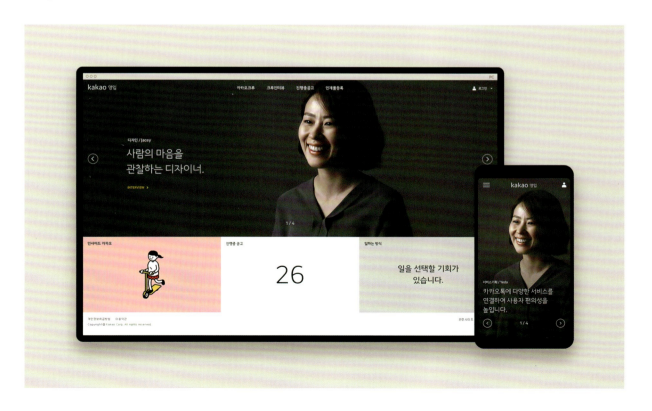

Sunday

Design Agency/ **Robot Food**

Sunday is a conceptual idea for a new pension brand to disrupt what many find to be a confusing and complicated category. In response to the brief provided by Robot Food, Sunday's aim was to rethink and reposition pensions, encouraging a proactive and positive approach to saving through a youthfully upbeat visual style and tone. To create the brand mark, the studio took inspiration from deconstructed pie charts, bringing to life the literal building blocks of a secure financial future. The brand itself was inspired by new-gen fintech with illustrations and photography reflecting the lifestyle of an audience looking to plan their futures.

Official

Behance

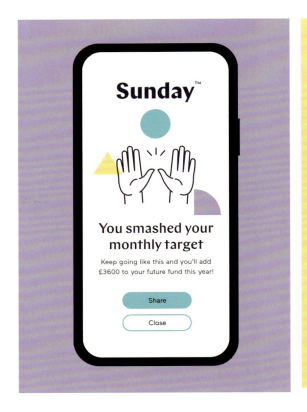

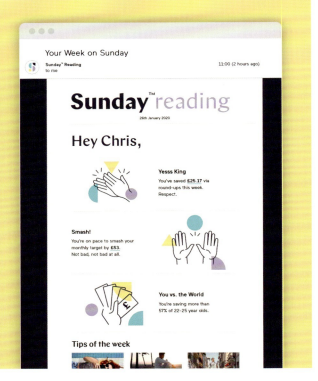

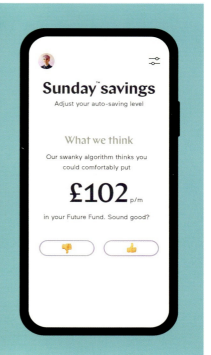
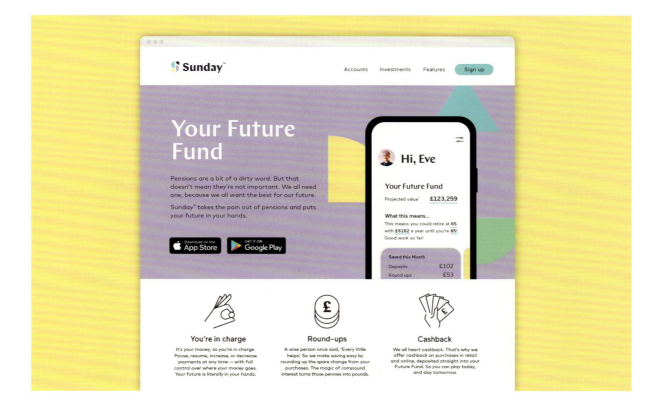

Aqer

Design/ **Luca Fontana**

Aqer is a ground-breaking video content platform where influencers and brands can create advertising campaigns together. Here the "A" in the logo is suggestive of an arrow directed towards growth. Luca Fontana created a website that is consistent with this promise by using futuristic design and dynamic navigation that is tilted towards content. And the modern blocks of solid colors meet the tastes of influencers and creative companies. He designed a visual identity consistent with the principles of simplicity and dynamism, which transformed Aqer into a perfect meeting place where influencers and brands can forge new, smart partnerships.

Official

Behance

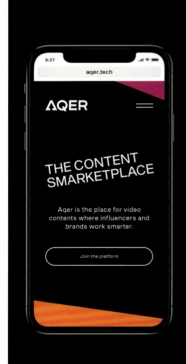

Nommi.net

Design/ **Aldiyar**

Inspired by the illustrations on Behance and Shopify, Aldiyar designed new version of icons for the app Nommi. The new icons accurately display the multiple functions of this app, such as the purchase of data packages and viewing charts.

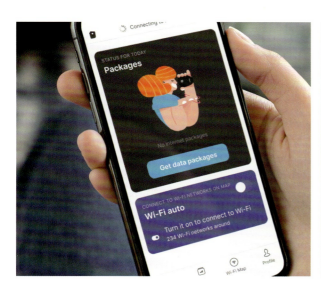
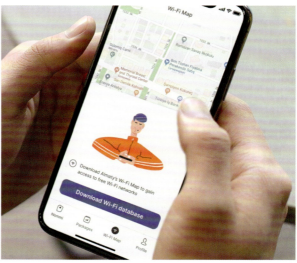

Sooner

Design Agency/ **Firmorama**

Sooner is a modern and welcoming brand that stands out in the investment market and can express itself easily. Firmorama used a simple and bright color palette for the key visuals and iconography. The app can easily help its clients fulfill their desires in the investing market.

Official

Tofu Design Website

Design Agency/ **Tofu Design Studio**
Design/ **Daniel Tan**
Copywriting/ **Daphnie Loong**

Inspired by tofu, Tofu Design Studio trickled this idea into the website and branding design. They wanted the website to look clean, smooth and easy to digest while pairing well with any color palette. They also designed a set of icons so everyone who visits their website will know how to navigate and understand it.

Behance

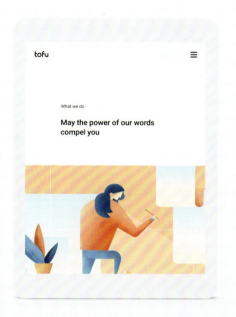

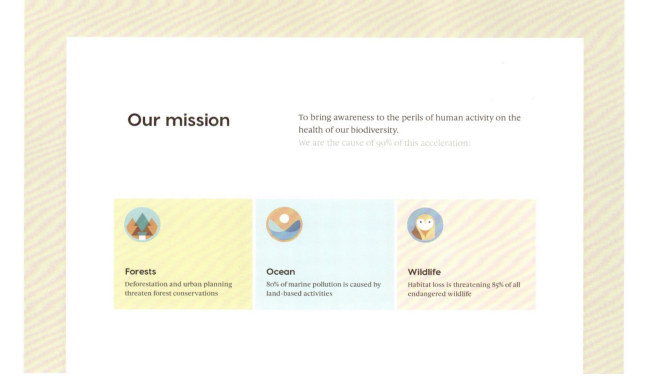

Rakfice

Design Agency/ **enhanced Inc.**
Client/ **PERSOL INNOVATION CO., LTD.**

Starting in 2019, enhanced Inc. has provided Rakfice logo construction, logo guideline development, UI/UX design of the website, product design and art direction for various sales tools. They designed a light blue icon set reminiscent of the sea for Rakfice's logo. In May 2020, Rakfice service officially launched and has been steadily gaining users of its services.

Official

Behance

DNB Lærepenger

Icon Design/ **Martine Lindstrøm**
Art Direction/ **Håkon Meyer Stensholt, Morten Johansen**
Cooperation/ **ANTI**
Client/ **DNB, The Norwegian Bank**

Money is becoming increasingly more abstract now that most payments are made invisibly by card or online transfers. The Norwegian Bank launched the app DNB Lærepenger, which aims to teach children more about the economy and money. While using the DNB brand colors, Martine Lindstrøm designed a set of friendly icons to add playfulness to the app and to speak to a young audience.

Behance

SBI Bank App

Design Agency/ **Mish Design Lab**
Art Direction/ **Marina Pimenova, Ivan Krestov**
Illustration/ **Anna Batalova**

Mish Design Lab's task was to design a bank app for the whole family. In the design, they reflected children and adult's apps and provided a new idea for the market—family banking. They aimed for symbols that are well accepted by adults, but, at the same time, attractive to children. As a result, the icons are simple symbols with curves as if they were drawn by a child. This allowed the design team to preserve the clarity of the image.

Behance

   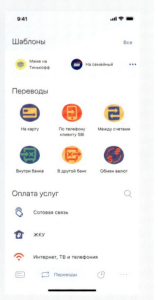

KNVB—Royal Dutch Football Association

Design Agency/ **Momkai**
Design/ **Harald Dunnink, Martijn van Dam, Tom Somers, Lukas Kouwets**

KNVB serves a broad range of people, from players to trainers, from club directors to referees. Such an organization called for a broad but crystal clear communication platform. Momkai designed the platform www.knvb.nl with a straightforward visual language. Incorporating a range of icons that speak to visitors with different backgrounds and roles within their clubs, Momkai used visual cues from both on and off the pitch.

Official

Behance

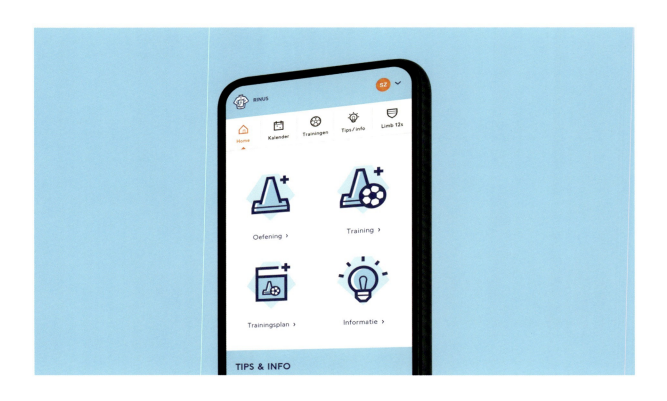

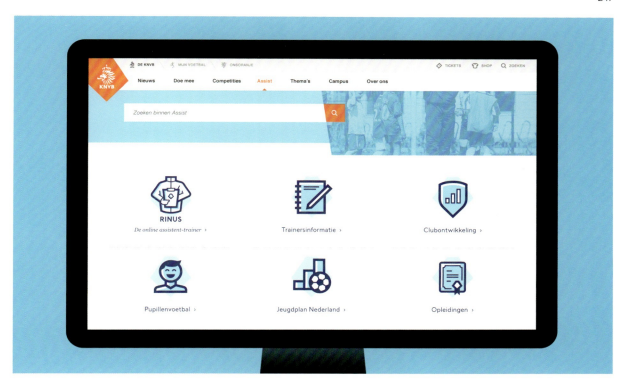

Made X Made— Website

Design Agency/ **Made Somewhere**

Made Somewhere was tasked to create an engaging and user-friendly e-commerce website for Made X Made that customers could use to discover, browse, purchase and download from thousands of icons and hundreds of collections. Made Somewhere created a friendly and approachable brand that captured the essence of Made X Made and reflected this across a functional and welcoming website.

Official

Behance

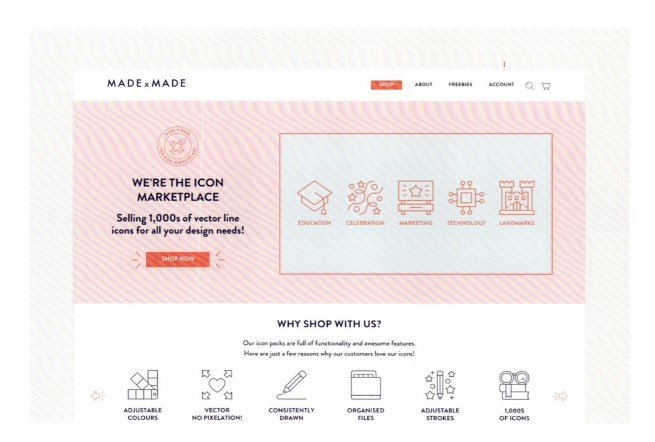

3% Design Studio
behance.net/zlyx

3% Design Studio is a design agency focusing on branding, illustrations, picture books and handmade artworks.

P052

6D-Kco., Ltd.
www.6d-k.com

6D is a graphic design agency based in Japan.

P046-047

702design
www.by702.com

702 is an experimental visual design institution. 702 has been fronting the design industry with its experimental approach and vision in innovation.

P136-137

Aldiyar
aidash.kz

Aldiyar is a designer based in Kazakhstan.

P237

Alejandra Melo Plaza
behance.net/alejandramelo

Alejandra Melo Plaza is a graphic designer and freelance photographer focusing on packaging and branding.

P158-159

Aleksandra Lampart
alelampart.pl

Aleksandra Lampart is a graphic designer based in Poland.

P034

Anastasiia Mysliuk
behance.net/anastasiia_mysliuk

Anastasiia Mysliuk is an economist by profession and a web designer in the soul.

P229

André Panoias, Miguel Muralha
behance.net/apanoias
behance.net/pardalsart

André Panoias and Miguel Muralha are two designers based in Portugal.

P119

Anna Giedryś, Peter Machaj
ancymonic.com

Anna Giedryś and Peter Machaj are a Polish–Slovak designer duo.

P118

Antonay
behance.net/ntnay

Antonay is a graphic designer and illustrator based in San José, Costa Rica.

P104-105

Arata Takemoto Design
www.takemotodesign.com

Arata Takemoto Design is a design firm active and based in Tokyo, Japan. They focus on environmental graphics and are also active in various fields of design.

P186-187

Assembly Studio
assemblystudio.co.za

Assembly Studio was founded by Jean-Paul Brouard, based in Durban, South Africa.

P226-227

Atemporal Agency, Hermes Mazali, Luis Fasah
www.atemporal.agency
hmazali.com
luisfasah.com

Atemporal is an independent brand design and experience agency, focusing on bringing companies, products and organizations closer to people through design, strategy and simplicity.

Hermes Mazali is a graphic designer and art director based in Barcelona, Spain. He focuses on creative, strategic and holistic solutions for companies, brands and agencies around the world.

Luis Fasah is freelance graphic designer based in Buenos Aires, Argentina.

P170-171

AURØRA Design
auroradesign.is

AURØRA is a creative design studio focusing on branding, UI/UX design and communication experiences that connect with people and emotionally engage them.

P114

Bearfruit Idea
www.bearfruitidea.com

Bearfruit Idea is a team that designs all icons with the highest attention to detail. Their icons are geometric, consistent, clean and fresh.

P013

Bedow
www.bedow.se

Bedow is a design agency that builds design solutions for innovators, artists and organizations with rationality, craft and ingenuity. The results are progressive, enduring and engaging.

P077

BIS Studio Graphique

behance.net/bisstudio

BIS Studio Graphique is a graphic design studio based in Toulouse, France.

P038-039

Blank Studio

www.studioblank.pl

Blank Studio is a multi-award winning design studio from Tychy, Poland. It is one of the few companies in Poland and Europe that specializes exclusively in designing complex wayfinding systems for various public spaces.

P128-129, P194-195

Bleed Design Studio

bleed.com

Bleed blurs design, technology, art and strategy to create compelling visual identities, services and experiences for their clients.

P108-109

Büro Destruct

www.burodestruct.net

Büro Destruct is a Switzerland-based design studio keeping open the boundary between art and commercial graphic design.

P134

Busybuilding

www.busybuilding.com

Busybuilding is a multidisciplinary branding and design agency based in Athens, Greece. The agency's diverse team consists of creatives and technologists who work and think together to build great brands.

P035

Bwow Studio

www.bwowstudio.com

Bwow Studio is a digital product design studio based in Spain.

P232

Caparo Design Crew

www.caparo.gr

Caparo Design Crew is a design-led creative agency. The designers in the studio do what they love and build brands that can top their potential, inspire people and add to the goodness of this world.

P076

Chiara Marchiori

chiaramarchiori.com

Chiara Marchiori is a multidisciplinary designer with over six years of experience in a variety of creative industries. She enjoys creating and innovating solutions for UI/UX, illustrations, branding, storyboarding and animations.

P118

Christina Boletus

behance.net/christinaboletus

Christina Boletus is a graphic designer based in Russia.

P058-059

Cristian Garske

cristiangars.com

Cristian Garske is a forward-thinking and creative Brazilian designer specializing in UX and digital product development.

P120

Daigo Daikoku, Daikoku Design Institute

daikoku.ndc.co.jp

Daigo Daikoku entered Nippon Design Center after graduating from the Kanazawa College of Art in 2003 and started Daikoku Design Institute in 2011. He moved to Los Angeles in 2018. He has worked with companies, educational organizations, governments, architects and artists to create projects in various fields.

P188-189

Dave Arustamyan

behance.net/arustamyandave

Dave Arustamyan is a graphic designer from Armenia.

P110-111

DesignStudio

design.studio

DesignStudio creates brands the world loves.

P062-063

DIFT

www.dift.be

DIFT is a Belgium-based, award-winning creative agency.

P180-181

Dmitriy Mirolyubov

behance.net/dmitriymir

Dmitriy Mirolyubov is a designer based in Russia.

P205

Elisabetta Calabritto

www.elisabettacalabritto.com

Elisabetta Calabritto is a graphic designer, illustrator and icon designer based in Italy.

P204-205

enhanced Inc.

enhanced.jp

enhanced Inc. was founded in 2012 by Hiromi Maeo, a Japanese graphic designer with over 20 years of experience.

P242-243

Familia

www.byfamilia.com

Familia is a graphic design studio that works with groups of typefaces, colors, materials, formats, solutions and people with experience in the fields of graphic identities, editorial design, packaging, websites and apps.

P036-037

Firmalt

www.firmalt.com

Firmalt is a branding and storytelling agency based in Mexico. They design brands that get lots of attention, love and profits.

P074-075

Firmorama

firmorama.com

Firmorama is a design agency based in Jaraguá do Sul, Brazil.

P117, P238–239

flat-icons.com

flat-icons.com

flat-icons.com is a team that brings pixel-perfect icons to the world from Amsterdam, the Netherlands.

P011, P203

Forma

forma.co

Forma is a graphic design and illustration studio based in Barcelona, Spain. They help people, companies and institutions to create or enhance their images. They always work with ideas as a starting point, using a clean and bold aesthetic.

P112, P130–131, P142–143

Frida Medrano

fridamedrano.com

Frida Medrano is a Mexican type and digital designer living in San Francisco.

P086–087

Futura

www.byfutura.com

Futura is a creative studio and wants to change the world. They wish they could find the cure for cancer but they will not. Instead, they create great brands, provocative images, beautiful objects, comfortable spaces and user-friendly interfaces. That is their way of improving the quality of life for those they reach.

P082–083

Graphasel Design Studio

www.graphasel.com

Graphasel Design Studio is a design agency based in Hungary.

P200

Greco Design

grecodesign.com.br

Greco Design is a design agency in Belo Horizonte, Brazil.

P190–191

Gustav Karlsson Thors

www.gustavkarlsson.com

Gustav Karlsson Thors is a graphic and motion designer based in Sweden.

P053

Hanno van Zyl

hannovanzyl.co.za

Hanno van Zyl is an independent designer and illustrator who works from the collaborative studio space, Only Today in Cape Town, South Africa.

P100–101

Icons8, Marina Fedoseenko

icons8.com
dribbble.com/marina-f

Icons8 is a design studio that creates icons, vectors, photos, music and tools.

Marina Fedoseenko is an icon artist and illustrator.

P010

Imagine Branding Studio

imagine.lt/en

Imagine is a digital-driven branding studio in Vilnius, Lithuania. They provide brand strategy, creative and design service to a wide range of different scale clients.

P098–099

Indielogy

dribbble.com/indielogy

Indielogy is an independent graphic/icon designer from Bandung, Indonesia.

P010

Inplace

behance.net/estudioinplace

Inplace creates design projects that optimize the relationship between people and spaces. They work for spaces, transforming them into friendly, accessible and homey environments. Each space presents a new challenge, which invites Inplace to meet it, interpret it and give it voice.

P196–197

İrem Uyar

behance.net/iremuyar

İrem Uyar is a freelance graphic designer and illustrator from Istanbul, Turkey.

P183

iStar Design Bureau

istardesign.com

iStar Design Bureau is a creative agency focusing on websites and UI/UX design, branding and graphic design.

P016

Jihee Kim, Jiyou Park

behance.net/Jiheeeee
behance.net/gziyou

Jihee Kim is a UI/UX designer based in South Korea. She designs to make people's daily lives more lively and convenient.

Jiyou Park is a designer based in New York, USA.

P228

József Balázs-Hegedűs

www.balazshegedus.com

József Balázs-Hegedűs is a freelance graphic designer and illustrator from Romania, living in Budapest, Hungary. He started his freelancing career as a web designer, but slowly shifted toward infographics, custom icon design, geometric and isometric illustrations.

P014

Kanda Euatham

www.becrisdesign.com

Kanda Euatham is a graphic designer based in Thailand.

P015

KARAPPO Inc.
karappo.net

KARAPPO is a design and consulting firm specializing in graphics, websites and user interface design. KARAPPO offers functionality, not just surface design, but fundamental design by planning the entire process of concept development, planning and system design.

P135

Kenneth Kuh
kennethkuh.info

Kenneth Kuh is an award-winning, transdisciplinary designer based in Los Angeles, Shanghai and Taipei.

P028-029, P050-051

Kerismaker Studio
facebook.com/kerismakerstudio

Kerismaker is a creative digital design studio in Indonesia focusing on icon design, illustrations and template design in collaboration with several marketplaces around the world. Kerismaker Studio was established in 2010 and has a lot of experience with various design needs.

P203, P207, P208

Kissmiklos
kissmiklos.com

Kissmiklos' works incorporate various facets of architecture, fine art, design and graphic design. A strong artistic approach and outstanding aesthetic quality characterize his art. His fine art pieces are as significant as his distinctive style in corporate identities and graphic design.

P017-025

KittoKatsu
www.kittokatsu.de

KittoKatsu is a small agency specializing in brand strategy and design. It works with a broad range of clients from individuals and institutions, to local businesses and global brands. The studio believes in strong brand management as the foundation for good design.

P042-043

Kolektyf
www.kolektyf.com

Kolektyf is a design studio based in Poland, specializing in creating wayfinding systems, mural graphics and infographics.

P115, P162-165

LIE
www.wearenotlie.com

LIE is an acronym of "Little Ideas Everyday." It's an independent graphic design studio based in Kuala Lumpur, Malaysia. Founded in 2011, LIE works across a diverse range of visual communication projects. They constantly practice and seek fresh approaches, and provide innovative and beautiful solutions for clients as well as self-initiated projects.

P168-169

Luca Fontana
fontanaluca.com

Luca Fontana is a freelance graphic designer based in Treviso, Italy, specializing in visual identities, web design and graphic design systems with a modern and aesthetic approach.

P236

Made Somewhere
madesomewhere.com.au

Made Somewhere is a creative studio based in Sydney, Australia. Working with local and international clients, they span a wide range of graphic design services from branding and packaging to digital and print design.

P248

Makers Company
www.themakers.company

Makers Company is a creative duo based in Cape Town, South Africa, who believes good design simplifies life, communicates across borders and beautifies the world. The studio shares a passion for building relationships and working in a collaborative environment to make great stories come to life for their clients and friends.

P220-221

Marin Gorea Jr.
instagram.com/maringoreajr

Marin Gorea Jr. is a professional graphic design freelancer from Moldova.

P096-097

Marta Gawin
www.martagawin.com

Marta Gawin is a multidisciplinary graphic designer specializing in visual identity, communication, poster, exhibition, sign systems, book and editorial design. Her design approach is conceptual, logical and content-driven. She treats graphic design as a field of visual research and experiments.

P116

Martine Lindstrøm
behance.net/martinemaya7f4a

Martine Lindstrøm is a Norwegian freelance designer based in Germany.

P244

Masaki Hanahara
www.masakihanahara.com

Masaki Hanahara started his career at SHISEIDO as a graphic designer in 2005. He was in charge of branding SHISEIDO and MAQuillAGE and of SHISEIDO's corporate advertising. In recent years, his works have expanded from general graphic design to interactive design, transcending the media's borders. He presented the IoT product and app at SXSW in 2017. Two of his poster series were selected by the national museum in Poland for its official collection in 2019.

P172-173

Mateo Flandoli
www.dflandoli.com

Mateo Flandoli is a designer based in Ecuador.

P144-145

Metric

www.metricdesign.no

Metric provides businesses in all sectors with any design-related challenges, big or small. Their services include identity, brand strategy and design, packaging, wayfinding system, digital design and concept development for any media or platform.

P132-133, P154-157

Microdot Graphic

dribbble.com/microdotgraphic

Microdot Graphic is a design studio that creates consistent, pixel-perfect and unique icons for creative design.

P206-207, P208

Mish Design Lab

mish.design

Mish Design Lab is a Moscow-based studio focusing on UI/UX design for the financial sector.

P245

Momkai

momkai.com

Momkai is a design studio that helps dreamers and thinkers build brands and platforms that serve a purpose.

P246-247

Monkik

behance.net/monkik

Monkik is a graphic designer, specializing in illustration and icon design, based in Chiang Mai, Thailand.

P202

Mountteam

www.mountteam.ru

Mountteam is an independent design team. They specialize in the development of trademarks, corporate identities, packaging, editorial and environmental design.

P030-031

MuchaDSGN

www.muchadsgn.com

MuchaDSGN is a design studio based in Poland.

P140-141

My Creative

wearemycreative.com

My Creative is a Scottish, award-winning, creative agency, founded by designer Ewan Leckie.

P089

Nofrontiere Design GmbH

www.nofrontiere.com

Nofrontiere Design GmbH is a design agency that designs holistic and individual concepts and strategies to launch brands into the future and define their communication and visual language.

P072-073

Nusae

nusae.co

Nusae is a Bandung, Indonesia-based design studio focusing on creative graphic design, branding and environmental design with diverse experience and an eye for details.

P176-179

Pedro, Pastel & Besouro

www.pedro.studio

Pedro, Pastel & Besouro started in 2014 as a multi-arts lab focusing on handcrafted techniques to develop artistic and design projects. They believe drawing is the basis of the creative process to build illustrations, graphic design and animation projects.

P066-069

Pengguin

pengguin.hk

Pengguin is a multidisciplinary design studio based in Hong Kong, China, established in 2013 by the design duo—Todd & Soho. They believe good design should always give positive energy and visual satisfaction.

P084-085

Perky Bros

perkybros.com

Perky Bros exists to help brands gain clarity, value and distinction through design. They create visual identities, websites, packaging, prints and anything necessary to create an authentic experience.

P106-107

Platform 64 Design Studio

platform64.co.uk

Platform 64 is a versatile design studio with a unique sense of creativity. They work with brands and businesses—big and small—to bring out their unique voice by creating unseen and dynamic works.

P064-065

POINT OF REFERENCE Studio

behance.net/jeffreyludlow

POINT OF REFERENCE Studio is a design studio based in Madrid, Spain.

P174-175

POMPAA

pompaa.com

POMPAA is an Istanbul-based multidisciplinary design firm specializing in branding, visual identity, publication, exhibition, wayfinding and web design. In addition to design projects, POMPAA also researches and develops various interactive applications from apps to public space installations.

P192-193

Project On Museum

www.projectonmuseum.com

Project On Museum is a design and strategy team from Taiwan, China. Their team members are from different backgrounds such as graphic design, business and marketing.

P070-071

ReflexDesign

www.reflexdesign.cn

ReflexDesign is a design and innovation studio. The studio provides design and consultation services for customers in different industries.

P040-041

Repina Branding

repinabranding.ru

Repina Branding is a creative branding agency based in Moscow, Russia.

P102-103

Robot Food

www.robot-food.com

Robot Food is a strategic branding agency based in Leeds, UK.

P234-235

Ruitong Zhu

www.ruitongzhu.com

Ruitong Zhu is a Chinese visual designer and illustrator who is currently working in Toronto, Canada.

P224-225

Sägenvier DesignKommunikation

saegenvier.at

Sägenvier DesignKommunikation is a graphic design studio based in Dornbirn, Austria.

P138-139

Sagmeister & Walsh

sagmeisterwalsh.com

Sagmeister & Walsh is the design partnership of Stefan Sagmeister & Jessica Walsh. Together, they create self-initiated creative arts projects.

P026-027

Savelii Shirokov

behance.net/savashi

Savelii Shirokov is a product designer based in Russia.

P222-223

Scandinavian Design Group

www.sdg.no

Scandinavian Design Group is a design agency based in Norway.

P060-061, P152-153

Seungtae Kim

behance.net/blackim80

Seungtae Kim is a freelance designer based in South Korea.

P233

Siwat Vatatiyaporn

iconfinder.com/antto

Siwat Vatatiyaporn works as a UI designer based in Bangkok, Thailand.

P016

SKG

s-k-g.net

SKG is a design agency based in Japan.

P150-151, P160-161

Smalllike

iconfinder.com/smalllike

Smalllike is a designer based in Thailand.

P013, P202

Stéphanie Aubin

stephanieaubin.com

Stéphanie Aubin is a graphic designer and illustrator living in Montreal, Canada.

P167

Studio Wete

studiowete.com

Studio Wete is a small and independent graphic design studio based in Barcelona, Spain that loves typography, graphic design and illustration.

P048-049

studiowmw

studiowmw.com

studiowmw is a multidisciplinary design studio based in Hong Kong, China and founded in 2013. They create branding, prints, products, packaging, exhibitions, installations and websites.

P092-093

SUAN Conceptual Design

suan.ch

SUAN is a team of visionaries, futurists, designers and doers. They seek to understand, imagine and express complicated concepts in simple, light and captivating artwork.

P182

the branding people

tbpmx.com

the branding people is a design studio based in Mexico City, specializing in branding and the development of visual communication systems.

P078-079

The Woork Co

www.thewoork.co

The Woork Co is a Madrid-based branding studio. The studio helps brands find their reason why, stories, images and voices.

P057, P214-215

Tofu Design Studio

www.tofudesign.co

Tofu Design Studio is a creative studio that provides solutions for companies with meaningful missions.

P240-241

Tom Birch

behance.net/birchplease

Tom Birch is a graphic designer living and working in the UK. Currently, his focus is on creating concept-led modern brands, which aim to combine design with culture to build meaning and connect with people in unexpected ways.

P209-213

Touch

thetouchagency.co.uk

Touch is an independent Scottish design studio. They have grown a great deal over the years while staying small enough to focus on doing what they do best.

P080-081

Turkkub

iconfinder.com/turkkub

Turkkub is a Thai icon designer.

P015

Tyodi Hyojin Lee, Hyunwoo Kim

behance.net/tyodi
behance.net/iam_kimhyunwoo

Tyodi Hyojin Lee is a brand experience designer in Seoul, South Korea. He attempts to deliver the differentiated brand experience by boundlessly agonizing about the various intersections of brand and customers.

Hyunwoo Kim is a brand experience designer in Seoul, South Korea.

P032-033

ujidesign

ujidesign.com

ujidesign is a design studio based in Tokyo, Japan.

P198-199

Ulkar Nasibova

behance.com/ulnasib

Ulkar Nasibova is an Azerbaijani designer with innovative ideas and a unique approach to visuals.

P094-095

Un Barco

www.unbarco.com

Un Barco is a creative studio based in Argentina, founded in 2014 and led by Josefina Hernalz Boland and Tomás Fernandez Treviño.

P056

Underline Studio

underlinestudio.com

Underline Studio takes on a wide range of projects in brands, digital corporates and marketing communications. The studio is global in its outlook and tastes, blending classic and emerging design thinking in work across the private and public sectors.

P216-217

Uniforma

uniforma.pl

Uniforma is a motion, branding and web design creative studio founded in 2007. The studio operates in various fields of visual communication using a wide range of digital technologies, often collaborating with other designers.

P166

Universal Favourite

universalfavourite.com.au

Universal Favourite is a Sydney-based brand and digital design consultancy with refreshingly insightful people and design, crafting beautiful award-winning solutions.

P054-055, P218-219

UVMW

uv-warsaw.com

UVMW is a design agency based in Poland.

P146-149

Victor Gorovoy

behance.net/vitya5000

Victor Gorovoy is a UI/UX designer based in Russia.

P230-231

Wander

designwander.studio

Wander is founded by Wik Kee Y. in 2016. It's currently based in Petaling Jaya, Malaysia.

P090-091

XIEXIE DESIGN

xiexiedesign.cn

XIEXIE DESIGN is a design studio based in three cities in China—Shenzhen, Dongguan and Guangzhou.

P088

Yiğit Karagöz, TBWA Istanbul

www.yigitkaragoz.com
www.tbwa.com.tr

Yiğit Karagöz is a Turkish visual artist, senior art director and illustrator who makes commercials, large-scale integrated campaigns, graphic design projects and illustration projects. Previously, he worked as a creative group head at TBWA Istanbul.

P044-045

Yoshiaki Irobe, Irobe Design Institute

irobe.ndc.co.jp

Yoshiaki Irobe is a designer and art director who leads the Irobe Design Institute and is a member of the board of directors of the Nippon Design Center Inc. He designs across a broad spectrum, applying his graphic design techniques with his editorial perspective, from 2D/3D graphics to spatial design.

P121-127

Yunjung Seo

behance.net/yunjungseo

Yunjung Seo is a UI and graphic designer based in South Korea.

P012

Zuzanna Opozda

behance.net/zopozda542b

Zuzanna Opozda is a graphic designer based in Krakow, Poland. She is an iron award winner of the A' Design Award and Competition.

P184-185

ACKNOWLEDGMENTS

We would like to express our gratitude to all of the designers and studios for their generous contributions of images, ideas and concepts. We are also very grateful to many other people whose names do not appear in the credits, but who have made specific contributions and provided support. Without them, the successful compilation of this book would not have been possible. Special thanks to all of the contributors for sharing their innovation and creativity with all of our readers around the world.